Secret
^{To} Happy
Children
& grandchildren

if they are small. . .give them roots
if they are big. . .give them wings

by Carl Metzger, M.D.

Carl Metzger, M.D. is a child, adolescent and adult psychiatrist actively involved in his private practice in the state of Maine. He received his M.D. in 1968 and holds Child Psychiatry fellowships from St. Luke's Hospital Center, N.Y., and Emory University, Atlanta, Georgia. He is a member of the American Psychiatric Association and the American Academy of Child and Adolescent Psychiatry.

Dr. Metzger is married and is the proud and caring parent of six beautiful and loving children, and two adorable grandchildren.

Published by: The Magni Group, Inc.
                P.O. Box 849
                McKinney, Texas 75070

Printed in the U.S.A.

ISBN No.: 1-882330-64-1

Website: www.magnico.com
E-mail: info@magnico.com

THE GOOD PARENTING GUIDE

Table of Contents

TO YOU, THE PARENTS AND GRANDPARENTS

Welcome to "**The Secret to Happy Children and Grandchildren**." Raising a child, listening to a child and responding to a child are all easier when you know what your child or grandchild needs and what his or her behavior means.

This book will help you know the "Secret" of good parenting and grandparenting and thereby insure a happy child. It will provide direction, instill confidence and increase understanding. Too often I have heard parents and grandparents wish for more understanding of their child's/grandchild's behavior. They know they can best respond to, and manage, a child's behavior, when they know why it is there in the first place.

Alternately, even when parents or grandparents have a sense of why their child or grandchild is behaving in a certain way, they would like to know exactly what to do (or what not to do) to keep their child/grandchild comfortable and to insure the best childhood development.

Through many years of working with children and counseling their parents, I have been greatly impressed by the "power" of parental love and good care. Grandparents can also share in this power. It is a power that insures that children/grandchildren develop comfortably and, if used fully, can keep children/grandchildren from trying or repeating "bad" behavior.

In this "**The Secret to happy Children and Grandchildren**," when I speak of "controlling behavior," using "firm, emotional responses," or showing "emotional displeasure," I am encouraging the use of this power as the primary consequence for bad, unacceptable, or testing behavior. Other consequences—behavioral or restrictive—are not necessary.

The behaviors presented here are very common. All children are involved with most of them.

There are several basic themes that appear repeatedly in this book, in one form or another; you can become familiar with them as a parent or grandparent. Although the "What Not to Do" and "What to Do" sections of each topic are written for a child's parent(s), grandparents can reinforce, support and even apply these principles themselves.

- Your child/grandchild does not want to feel like a "bad" boy or girl.

- Your child/grandchild wants you to be strong enough, and to know enough, to require good behavior.

- Feeling "bad" makes a child angry, depressed, and likely to continue repeating or escalating the bad behavior, in the hope that you will stop him or her.

- Your child's/grandchild's behavior results from a combination of developmental stage, circumstances, and how you, the parents/grandparents, are perceived by your child.

- It is never too late to do the right thing for your child/grandchild who is always waiting, and hoping, that you will.

All children want to feel that they are good and that you, their parents and grandparents, know how to provide the best care. "The Secret to Happy Children and Grandchildren" will help your child/grandchild feel comfortable, because it will help you feel like a knowledgeable and strong parent or grandparent.

DR. CARL METZGER
Portland, Maine

ACADEMIC DIFFICULTIES
Under Age 12

Discussion:

Consistent academic achievement not only implies a fair-to-good IQ, but also good communication, relative freedom from anxiety or depression, a certain amount of competitiveness, a desire to please, and a wish to maintain self-esteem. Impairment or lack in any of these areas can result in academic difficulties.

Efforts to assess and correct these difficulties should, therefore, involve a number of professional "experts," educators, administrators, and mental health professionals.

The longer academic difficulties continue, the harder they are to assess and correct.

A child's opinion of self-worth, both in the present and for the future, is strongly influenced by academic achievement.

A low level of academic achievement can significantly influence the child's social behavior and choice of friends — both with potentially long-lasting consequences.

Sudden academic difficulty is an important signal of some significant stress.

What Not to Do:

Don't overlook important and early warning signs: depressed mood in relation to school, resistance to school and schoolwork, reports of classroom behavior that is unusual for your child (sloppiness, inattention, withdrawing, or disruptive classroom behavior).

Don't hesitate to make immediate contact with the teacher if you have any doubts about your child's academics.

Don't expect your child to know why the difficulty exists.

Don't neglect contributing medical difficulties (illness, eye or ear troubles, alcohol/drug use, etc.).

Don't link academic difficulties to future insecurity, unhappiness, etc., in your child's mind – it might only increase the stress.

Try not to make academic difficulty a "punishable offense." It is probably too complex for that type of response.

What to Do:

Let your child know immediately that you view any academic decline very seriously.

If you have any idea of possible contributing stresses or circumstances, let your child know that you are aware of them.

Let your child know that you are in contact with the teachers.

Try reviewing your child's work in a quiet, comfortable setting, as free as possible from anger or frustration.

Seek professional mental health consultation if your efforts and the school professionals' responses don't seem to be working, if the pattern of academic difficulties intensifies rapidly, or if there is obvious depression or significant anxiety.

ACADEMIC DIFFICULTIES
Adolescents

Discussion:

Academic success at this age implies a good intellect, reasonable emotional comfort, established academic routine and some sense of future goals, as well as society's value on achievement.

It is much harder to deal with (and correct) long-standing academic difficulty than sudden recent academic difficulty.

Correcting such difficulty at this age often requires professional mental health consultation, so that contributing emotional and social stresses can be identified and corrected.

A particularly serious consequence of this difficulty is the possibility of the child's seeking a peer group of lower academic achievers – and the undesirable attitudes and behavior that commonly accompany such association.

Parents tend to feel helpless, because by this age there is little regular contact with teachers (more than one, now) and unfamiliarity with many of the academic subjects.

Attempts by parents to enforce study routines through the use of restrictions, etc., are often unsuccessful, because they are also restrictive of the child's social activities and so are strongly resented and resisted.

What Not to Do:

Don't be casual about any new pattern of lower academic achievement or impaired study effort.

Don't use restrictions that cover long periods of time and are not directly related to study time.

Don't threaten your child with long-term consequences having to do with jobs, earning power, or "success," as these issues already account for much of the stress your adolescent is experiencing.

Don't neglect contributing medical difficulties (illness, eye or ear troubles, alcohol/drug use, etc.).

What to Do:

Explain to your child that you are aware of the difficulty, that pride in academic achievement and capabilities is the goal you are working together to achieve.

Encourage your child to study and do homework in a room that is part of, or close to, family activity. A child closed off in a room won't necessarily work effectively.

Arrange consultation with your child's teachers, counselors, etc., quickly and frequently. Their awareness of your interest and concern may help the situation in important ways.

Remember that an academic "turnaround" can be exceedingly slow, but your expressed confidence that it will happen is crucial for your child.

ACCIDENT-PRONE

Discussion:

Accident-prone behavior exists when a child seems to have more than a fair share of accidents and when behavior makes accidents likely.

This can be a sign of depression in a child.

It can be caused by physical or perceptual difficulties (i.e., slight neurologic problems, visual problems). Make sure to mention accident-prone behavior to the child's physician or pediatrician.

This can be considered a dangerous difficulty, as there is a chance of serious injury to the child.

Over a long period of time, being accident-prone can contribute to low self-confidence and undesirable sense of vulnerability.

What Not to Do:

Don't punish your child. Parent(s) who were treated harshly for having accidents, themselves, may find it hard to resist punishing accident-prone children.

Don't give your child an "accident-prone" label or in any other way indicate that accidents are expected.

Don't overdo the sympathy you show. Too much may reinforce the behavior.

Don't try to modify the difficulty by the overuse of caution and warnings.

Don't restrict your child from appropriate activities in an attempt at protection.

What to Do:

Pay attention to activities, times of the day, or the company of certain children to establish whether there are patterns of these accidents. If there are, let the child know about them.

Give sympathy (in appropriate amounts) for the actual pain or injury suffered by your child, not for the mere fact of the accident.

Watch for other symptoms of depression (sad mood, withdrawal, sleep disturbance, impaired appetite, decreased school performance, negative feelings about self, etc.).

Encourage your child to describe exactly what led up to the accident. This gives your child more of a feeling of control, knowing you are capable discussing it, and may develop your child's innate sense of caution.

Seek professional mental health consultation if being accident-prone results in, or threatens to result in, serious injury, danger, obvious loss of confidence, or change in usual activities.

ACHES and PAINS
Ages 5-11

Discussion:

It can be difficult to determine whether aches and pains are "real" or psychological.

Even if they are psychological, the child can truly be in distress and "feel" the aches and pains.

Children are prone to experience aches and pains at certain developmental stages.

Success in eliminating this difficulty rests largely with the parents' response and how the child perceives that response.

"Headaches" and "stomachaches" are the most common kinds of psychologically related aches and pains.

These aches and pains tend to occur repeatedly in certain situations or at certain times (school, bedtime, etc.).

What Not to Do:

Don't hesitate to have your child evaluated by the family pediatrician or physician. You will respond more effectively if you are sure in your own mind that your child is medically well.

Don't accuse your child of "faking" or "imagining" the aches and pains.

Don't ask often or repeatedly how your child is feeling.

Don't respond with anger toward your child when he or she is complaining. (This can happen as a result of your frustration and even your fear of the situation.)

Don't ignore your child's complaints.

Don't change your child's routines or eliminate normal activities on the basis of the complaints.

What to Do:

Let your child know that you are hearing the complaints.

Sympathize with the fact that your child feels distress, but don't overdo it.

Follow sympathy quickly with the attitude, "Let's go on with life as usual."

Seek professional mental health consultation if your responses and handling of your child don't seem to be working, and especially if certain routines become affected or interrupted (play, bedtime, school, etc.).

ACHES and PAINS
Adolescents

Discussion:

There is always a tendency for regression in the adolescent years. Aches and pains tend to provide the adolescent a convenient excuse for that regression.

As body changes are a hallmark of these years, psychological difficulties readily express themselves in body aches and pains.

It is easier to differentiate "real" from psychological aches and pains because of the child's increased ability to describe and detail them.

Headaches and stomachaches still predominate, but other common areas affected are limbs and back (and lower abdomen, specifically for menstruating girls).

As children in this age group are prone to certain "real" injuries or body pains (because of sports, horsing around, body building, menstruation) psychological aches and pains can develop from them quite easily.

What Not to Do:

Don't rule out real disease or injury. Discuss the problem with the family physician or pediatrician.

Don't accuse your child of "faking" or "imagining" the pain.

Don't accuse your child of "acting like a baby."

If possible, don't allow your child to change routine, eliminate responsibilities, or avoid situations because of the aches and pains.

What to Do:

Give sympathy and acknowledge what your child is

experiencing, according to what seems appropriate to you and according to the degree to which your child seems to want such a response from you.

Allow for private and serious discussion with your child, considering the possible stresses in life at that particular time.

Seek professional mental health consultation if your responses and handling don't seem to be working, or if you are aware of obvious depression or impaired functioning in your child.

ALCOHOL USE
Adolescents

Discussion:

Alcohol is very readily available, is heavily advertised, is addictive, and is a prevalent part of adolescent socialization – all reasons why its use can become a major difficulty during adolescence.

Parents' own mixed feelings about alcohol make dealing with alcohol use in their children difficult.

As with adults, alcohol can be used by adolescents to escape from, or cope with, stressful situations (yes, parties can be stressful).

Since alcohol is addictive, and since early patterns of addiction can lead to major trouble later, effective response to this behavior is extremely important.

Besides the psychological and functional consequences of alcohol use at this age, physical consequences can be very serious.

What Not to Do:

Don't forget that some experimentation with alcohol, as with other substances and activities during adolescence, is a natural expression of your child's developing independence, curiosity, etc.

Don't overlook or ignore any circumstances where your child is regularly using alcohol or is visibly intoxicated.

Don't hesitate to restrict or forbid the use of the car while a pattern of regular or heavy alcohol use is suspected.

Don't feel that you have to justify or conceal your own use of alcohol, (assuming it is reasonable and controlled). It is not hypocritical to point out that certain activities are appropriate only for certain ages.

What to Do:

As much as possible, express your concern, anger, disappointment, etc., to your child with regard to the alcohol use itself. Deliver a clear message of the unacceptibility of such behavior. However, if you also criticize those activities and peers that may be a part of the alcohol use, your message won't be as effective or as well received.

Every so often, ask your child if alcohol is a problem or ask to discuss alcohol use in general. You can learn a lot from the response.

Carefully watch for indications of alcohol use: mood changes, alcohol breath, slurred speech, extended sleep after being out at night, etc.

Consult a chemical dependency professional if alcohol use becomes regular; if your responses to this behavior don't work; if the child's physical health is threatened; or if there are other emotional difficulties causing, or consequent of, the alcohol use.

Consult with Alcoholics Anonymous or other community programs to determine if there are appropriate services available for your child and yourselves.

ANGER IN CHILDREN

Discussion:

Anger is a "reflex emotion." It exists when a child feels uncomfortable.

All children are entitled to moments, even hours, of anger. It is an inevitable part of developing and growing up.

The "angry child" is one who shows evidence of anger for long periods of time.

In general, the angry child perceives certain important needs as not being met, thereby leading to discomfort and to the anger.

Anger in a child can take the form of an angry mood or words, defiance, sullenness, silence and withdrawal, or persistent misbehavior.

An angry child, then, is one who needs a change in his or her relationship with the parents.

What Not to Do:

Don't "give up" on your child or express helplessness or return your child's anger with yours.

Don't punish your child for being angry, unless the anger presents itself in unacceptable behavior (screaming, throwing or breaking things, swearing). At this point, you can, at least, provide structure.

When you discover the reasons for your child's discomfort, don't expect the anger to clear suddenly and be gone. In fact, the anger will disappear, but at a slow and steady rate.

What to Do:

This is a potentially serious situation. It is serious because your child is uncomfortable, and serious because you would not have permitted the situation to get to this point if you had known what to do differently.

Feel free to ask your child to explain the anger that is present but don't expect he or she to easily respond. Ultimately, your child expects you to know what it is about and to do something to relieve it.

Accept the anger but be clear and consistent with your child regarding appropriate behavior with the expression of anger, i.e., "It is OK to say you are angry, but you cannot call one names."

You should consult someone knowledgeable in child development and, if necessary, a mental health professional.

ARGUING
Adolescents

Discussion:

True arguing is not possible before adolescence, because arguing takes a mind capable of logic, advanced knowledge, and adult-like expression. (In younger children, disagreement takes the form of protest.)

Arguing is a vital developmental activity. It allows for competition, a way of expressing independence, and a means of having closeness. (Intensity between two people, even negative, is a type of involvement.)

It is a rule that, as much as adolescents appear to need to argue with parents, they also need to lose most of these arguments, especially if the arguments involve issues of closeness, safety, or morality.

Arguments that go on for long periods of time or that become increasingly angry need to be ended immediately. In drawn-out arguments, your child experiences insecurity and anger, because of feelings that you are not strong enough to end (or win) the argument.

What Not to Do:

Don't accept behavior during an argument that you would not accept at other times (rudeness, swearing, or physical expressions of anger).

Likewise, don't show behavior, yourself, that is not up to your own standards.

Don't "put down" or attempt to outwit your child during the argument. Such behavior takes away from the developmental value of the arguing.

Don't feel that there is any time, or place, that is necessarily more appropriate for arguing. Engage in it and handle it. There will be times it will be more appropriate to finish the discussion at a different time – clearly indicate when that time will be.

What to Do:

Show your child that you have the confidence to argue a point, and then that you have the ability to end the argument.

AVOIDING PARENTS

Discussion:

Avoidance refers to those behaviors of the child that are calculated to ensure the child's privacy or to reduce anxiety.

This is a very specific condition and must be distinguished from testing or withdrawing behavior.

If handled correctly, the avoidance will be limited in time and type and won't lead to anger in either the child or the parents.

The avoidance may take the form of reduced communication, more time spent in private, or apparent discomfort with physical interaction.

This avoidance behavior typically occurs immediately following parental acts of discipline or anger; when private circumstances are necessary for a specific activity (a hobby that requires quiet or special surroundings, exercise, body building, band practice with friends, experimenting with makeup, etc.); when sexual development or anxiety require it (having an erection, wanting to masturbate, beginning menstruation, or for a girl, being around father when wearing a new or revealing type of clothing).

What Not to Do:

Don't comment to your child about the avoidance. It is best handled with quiet patience.

Don't let any anger that you experience about being avoided interfere with the proper management of the situation. Don't assume that avoidance means lack of love for you.

What to Do:

If you accidentally interfere with your child when he or she is avoiding you, just withdraw quietly.

BAD DREAMS
Under Age 3

Discussion:

These may occur occasionally or repeatedly.

The child will be screaming or crying furiously and will not seem to realize the parents are trying to be comforting.

A child's bad dreams can be upsetting to parents because of the child's apparent distress and the parents' difficulty in providing comfort.

Such dreams are more likely to occur if the child has had a tiring or "overstimulating" day.

What Not to Do:

Don't feel you have to calm your child at once. You will probably be in more apparent distress than your child during one of these episodes.

Don't yell loudly, shake, or slap in order to "wake" your child.

Don't stay around too long once your child is calmer and appears ready to resume sleep.

Don't expect your child to remember the episode the next day.

What to Do:

Sit next to your child, holding or hugging firmly, and keep talking in a reassuring way until your child is obviously calmer, no matter how long it takes.

BAD DREAMS
Over Age 3

Discussion:

To some degree these are a normal part of certain developmental stages.

However, bad dreams are of concern if they persistently interfere with good sleep patterns.

They are also of concern if your child seems to refer to them often during the day or if they become responsible for a fear of bedtime.

What Not to Do:

Don't expect your child to be willing or even able to recount the details of the dream or what it was about.

Don't push your child to talk about the dream if there is resistance to doing so.

Don't feel you have to restrict your child from watching horror movies or listening to or reading scary stories, unless you see a definite connection between these activities and the dreams.

Don't let your child's expressed fears of the dreams lead to the child's sleeping in your bed or your room or to you sleeping in your child's room.

What to Do:

Acknowledge your child's feeling of fear.

Give comfort briefly in the night, before firmly insisting on a return to bed.

Let your child know you are interested to hear about the dream.

Offer your child the opportunity to sit with you and draw pictures about the dream or play it out with puppets or dolls.

BED-SWITCHING BEHAVIOR
Young Children

Discussion:

This refers to the activity of spending all or part of the night in a bed (or beds) other than the child's own.

Sleep serves the important purpose of restoring the body and mind. It occurs in a dark room, usually separated from mother and father, which is a difficult combination for a young child.

Bed-switching starts when a child becomes aware of the dark, solitary situation and also knows that the parents are in a warm, soft bed of their own.

Bed-switching is a problem to the degree that: it interrupts the parents' or child's sleep; it occurs at a developmental stage when physical closeness with parents in bed is not good; or it comes to represent inconsistency and difficulty in establishing control on the part of the parent(s).

What Not to Do:

Don't "give in" one night and expect your child to stay in bed the next night. If you have made the decision to keep your child in his or her own bed, that decision must be carried out consistently.

Don't say that your child is bad, or that it is wrong to stay in your bed. Actually the less said, the better.

Don't try to correct this behavior by locking or shutting your child's door.

Don't try to correct this behavior by having mother or father go to your child's bed to sleep.

Don't warn your child in advance to stay in bed. Dealing with the behavior at the time it occurs is much more effective.

What to Do:

You can allow a brief "visit" to your bed occasionally. When it starts to become a regular activity, that is when it needs to be controlled.

An effective nonverbal technique is to make your child extremely uncomfortable in your bed by crowding almost to the edge, or by using your protruding elbow or knee.

Firmly tell the child to return to bed and stay there. If your child tests you by returning to your bed, 1) talk to your child, return with him or her to bed, briefly continue to talk, sit quietly for a few moments, and then quietly return to your bed or 2) an angry look or word can be used and, if necessary, a reasonable spank.

Bed-switching between siblings should be interrupted in the same way, if it becomes a problem.

BEDWETTING

Discussion:

This can be a sign of normal regression in the face of stress (actual or perceived) if it occurs once the child has a dry bed for six months or more.

If it occurs in an older child, it has more serious implications about stress (actual or perceived) and the child's ability to handle the stress.

It may have physical causes.

What Not to Do:

Don't assume immediately that there is a serious difficulty.

Don't shame your child, but don't ignore the fact that the bedwetting is happening.

What to Do:

Tell your child "this can happen sometimes." Acknowledge that the child is not bad for "bedwetting" and let the child know that if it continues you will attend to it.

Particularly with the older child, tell your child firmly, but not angrily, that you expect a stop to the bedwetting. Give praise extravagantly when you discover a dry bed in the morning.

Try to identify and attend to actual stress or try to elicit your child's perception of the stress (usually not easy to do).

If wetting becomes more than occasional, check first with your child's physician or pediatrician to rule out physical causes.

BITING
Ages 2-5

Discussion:

During these years, many of the child's activities and sensations involve the mouth. Therefore, considering all the other things the mouth is used for, it is not surprising that the child tries to use it as a weapon as well.

Since biting can really hurt, the victim will, no doubt, promptly and dramatically bring this behavior to your attention or to the attention of another adult.

This behavior must be dealt with immediately and effectively because biting can be dangerous. Other children quickly become frightened of a biter. The child must learn more appropriate ways of expressing anger.

What Not to Do:

Don't assume that removing your child from the situation is the only way of handling this behavior.

Don't encourage the other child (children) to bite your child back (you just might make biters out of them, too).

What to Do:

Show your child your disapproval and anger as soon as you observe or hear about the behavior.

Show your child the bite marks, redness, etc., that the bite has caused, and point out the pain of the other child.

Inflict appropriate physical pain on the child who bites to demonstrate how a bite can be painful (your child truly may not understand that teeth can cause pain).

BOSSINESS

Discussion:

Examples of this behavior are the child wanting his or her own way when playing with peers, or using physical means to intimidate or control peers.

When occasional or short-lived, this behavior can be a normal way for the child to test power with peers.

When this behavior occurs repeatedly, is sustained, and causes real distress to peers, it should be a cause for concern.

It is more likely to occur during stages of psychological growth when issues of power or fear are prominent.

Effective response to this behavior is important for the child's social education and for the child's sense of emotional comfort.

What Not to Do:

Don't interfere with this behavior if it has not become a real concern for you. There are advantages to letting children work these things out among themselves.

Don't restrict your child from friends or situations that are causing concern about bossiness, but rather, insist that your child change the behavior.

Don't worry that your interference will discourage competitiveness or your child's ability to hold his or her own. These qualities develop best in the child who is emotionally comfortable and sure of your guidance.

What to Do:

Call your child's attention to the behavior privately, but as soon as possible after the behavior appears.

Seek professional mental health consultation if your child is becoming isolated socially, is seriously hurting other children physically, or is emotionally over-involved with fear or the need to win.

BULLYING

Discussion:

This is primarily a behavior of boys, although it can certainly include girls – a way of competing physically, and through competing, gaining a sense of security.

It is a more serious behavior if it occurs individually rather than if it happens in a group.

A bully is a child who is both angry and feels vulnerable or insecure.

It is a behavior that feeds on itself. Authority figures and peers label the child as bad, and often they isolate him, thereby continuing the anger and the insecurity. Thus, unwittingly, they perpetuate the bullying they are trying to stop.

In very young children, aggressive social behavior is part of normal development – a way of learning about physical power and what behavior is possible with other children.

What Not to Do:

Except for very young children, don't bully your aggressive child back and don't encourage other children to bully him. This won't really "teach him a lesson."

Don't label your child as a "bully" or "bad."

Don't spend a lot of time asking why your child behaves this way. He really can't tell you.

If it is a group behavior, don't allow your child the excuse that "the other boys were responsible."

What to Do:

In a situation where your very young child pushes, kicks, or bites another child, firmly tell him not to do that. And if necessary you may have to use a moderate demonstration of bullying behavior with the bully to make more of an emotionally effective point (especially if the behavior seems resistant to your verbal responses). Be sure to tell the child this is a demonstration.

Tell the older child that you know he doesn't feel comfortable acting as he did and add firmly, with emotional power, not to do it again.

If the aggressive behavior seems likely to occur with the same group of boys, hold your child individually responsible and consider prohibiting his socializing with that group.

CARS and ADOLESCENTS

Discussion:

In adolescence, acquiring the ability to drive a car is probably the event that is most symbolic of independence. Never before this time has the child had the opportunity to go so far, so fast, in private.

As the issues of independence, separation, major responsibility, trust, and social availability all come into play in this car activity, it is not surprising that there is the potential for conflict and thus, behavioral problems.

Most adolescents are eager to get their driver's licenses. Some, sensing the potential conflict, show little or no interest in driving.

If all goes well, becoming a driver can lead to significant personal development. If all does not go well, there is a great potential for difficulty.

What Not to Do:

Don't postpone your child's getting a license if most of the children of the same age in your area are getting theirs.

As with other situations, don't assume your child will be bad (with frequent warnings or questions about car-related activities).

Don't present the car as a privilege. This has implications that there is an expectation of misbehavior, and hence, restrictions. As with anything else that your child is involved with, good behavior should be assumed.

If your child does abuse the car, violate your trust, or put anyone in danger, discipline effectively and emotionally. But don't take away the car.

Don't use indirect ways of postponing your child's driving for purposes of alleviating your own anxiety (making the child save up for insurance, waiting until the warmer weather, etc.).

What to Do:

Be excited about, and take an active part in, your child's lessons, permit, and license testing. This display on your part is a powerful message from you regarding your opinion of your child's competence, maturity, and trustworthiness.

Be available for lots of driving time with your child. Not only does this develop good driving skills, but also it makes you an important part of this major developmental milestone.

If your child uses the car for inappropriate social behavior, separation attempts, or risk-taking, attend to these problems as if there were no car involved. It is the issue that needs attention, not the vehicle with which it occurs.

If your child, as a driver, can be of assistance to you, assume so, as you would if there were no car involved.

If you can afford it, be free to offer gas money or to cover other necessary expenses. Your child expects this of you, just as he or she knows you would get a bike fixed, pay for the movies, etc. Just because a car is an adult object doesn't mean that your child no longer expects to be treated like a child.

CHEATING

Discussion:

Cheating is breaking or violating rules, expectations, or controls.

The label "cheating" also implies a deliberate and intentional behavior.

Cheating can be an expression of normal development when it is very limited, occurs at a young age, and serves the purpose of winning a competition and/or testing.

The older the child, and the more significant the context in which the cheating occurs, the more serious it is.

Serious cheating in children represents attempts to get needs met by acting badly with the hope that the cheating will be corrected.

Cheating must be corrected effectively in childhood to prevent cheating as an adult. Like other bad behavior, it fuels itself.

What Not to Do:

Don't think that anyone else can respond as effectively to your child's cheating as you can.

What to Do:

Consider consequences that range from a verbal apology to the person(s) involved to your firm, immediate, and emotional expressions of displeasure.

Be clear that you are responding to the cheating because it is bad behavior. The fact that other children don't like a cheater, or that cheating doesn't really get what your child is looking for, are logically correct, but they don't carry much emotional weight. Therefore they aren't very useful as a means of changing the behavior.

CIGARETTE SMOKING

Discussion:

When children need to feel or act older than their age for purposes of peer approval or to gain a feeling of security and strength, smoking is a common behavior. It is a visible behavior and one that children associate with adulthood.

It is also a behavior that lends itself easily to "doing wrong" (There are rules against it.); "being sneaky" (Cigarettes are small enough to be hidden, and, once the smoking has occurred there is little visible trace.); and "challenging authority" (Many children are determined not to be told what to do.).

As cigarettes are legal, available, and cheap, there is a good chance that most adolescents will come in contact with them.

What Not to Do:

Don't prohibit or ban smoking, unless you are prepared to enforce the ban. This means a firm response if you find cigarettes in drawers or purses, in the glove compartment of the car, etc.

Don't even get into the issue until there is good evidence that your child is smoking on a somewhat regular basis, or with some degree of frequency (some experimentation is a common necessary fact of adolescent development).

Don't think that a desire or effort to smoke is intended as self-destructive behavior. It usually has much more to do with the typical adolescent need to test and challenge and to be comfortable with peers.

What to Do:

Make it clear that you are prohibiting smoking because it is harmful to health and you will not allow your child to impair his or her own health. (If you smoke, yourself, don't worry about being a hypocrite. Parents are allowed to apply double standards in certain circumstances, simply because they are the parents.)

If, in fact, you have allowed your child to smoke, this is a mistake. There is no way your child can equate this with good parental care. But the mistake can be corrected. Simply say that you have decided it was not a good idea to allow smoking, since it is not healthful. It is not necessary or desirable to give any more reason for your change of mind.

CLINGING

Discussion:

"Clinging" takes place when a child can't seem to get enough affection; when what parents give doesn't seem to "do the trick"; when a child repeatedly gets in the parents' way and is starting to become a nuisance; when the child stays away from (or avoids) activities that ought to be more enjoyable than being with parents.

It can either be part of the normal developmental process, or it can signal that the child is having psychological difficulties.

Effective response not only helps the child's emotional development, but can also contribute greatly to the parents' relationship with the child.

The clinging sometimes is a nuisance to the parents because even the child does not find it natural or comfortable.

This behavior usually and naturally involves the mother more than the father.

What Not to Do:

Don't despair that your child has "gotten off the track of good development." Clinging is more of a refresher pause in that development.

Don't push your child away. This can make the clinging more intense and can impair your relationship with your child.

Don't call your child "a baby," "immature," etc. Your child already knows at some level that this behavior is regressive.

What to Do:

Be "receptive" to your child, even though it may involve being hugged, clinging, whining, etc.

After you have been receptive for a while (as long as circumstances permit, or your patience allows), disengage yourself by calling your child's attention to something else or naturally moving to another activity yourself.

If your child's age permits, put into words the fact that the child "needs some love," "needs a hug," etc., and identify or ask about anything stressful or difficult that is going on.

Seek professional mental health consultation if your responses, over time, do not seem to modify this type of behavior, or if this type of behavior interferes with important areas of your child's development.

COLLEGE ANXIETY

Discussion:

Whatever else it may represent to a child, the most significant meaning of the word "college" is leaving home. Therefore, it is not unusual for the high school student to resist talking or thinking about college.

Even as certain requirements of college choice or application become timely, parents may encounter tardiness, forgetfulness, or even anger on the part of their child.

Handling the college situation correctly is very important in assuring a comfortable, independent adjustment to the child's new situation outside the home.

The greater the child's unconscious "sense" that there is "unfinished business" left to do with parents, the more intense college anxiety is likely to be.

What Not to Do:

Don't bring up a lot of references to college before the child's junior year in high school. Your child is just not ready to process this information comfortably.

If your child is in the early teens and starts to bring up the issue of college (either talking a lot about going away to college or talking about not going to college at all), don't get into discussions or arguments. Rather, indicate that college is important, but that it is too early to do much talking about it.

Don't let your child feel alone with respect to reading about colleges, learning about the application process, setting up interviews, visiting, etc. You must be very heavily involved.

Don't feel that the final choice must truly be your child's alone. In fact, your input will help your child be most comfortable with whatever college is chosen.

Don't let your child limit choices, either in number or in quality.

Don't do a lot of comparisons, either to the college you went to or to the fact that you never had the opportunity to go to college (or complete it). This way, you avoid stirring up any anxiety based on conflicts about competing with you.

What to Do:

Make your feelings about the importance of college known in casual, occasional, and appropriate ways throughout your child's junior high and high school years.

At the beginning of the junior year in high school, start collecting and leaving around college guides and informational literature.

Make sure you are aware of the Scholastic Aptitude Test, achievement tests and application timetables, and post them for easy reference.

Respond to overtures your child makes regarding college discussion. But if there are no overtures well into the junior year, then initiate these discussions yourself.

When you recognize signs of anxiety, be free with the general interpretation that it must be hard, sometimes, to think about going off to college.

Be free with the occasional comment about how you will miss your child when he or she goes off to college.

COMPUTER USE

Discussion:

The computer presents a challenge to children of all ages. It will be a positive challenge if your child feels it can be learned and mastered, and if it provides knowledge and entertainment. It will be negative challenge if it is frustrating, overwhelming or allows bad behavior.

Changes and upgrades in computer components may led to confusion or inaction on the part of parents or grandparents.

Computer use can increase contact between family members and provide a way of sharing knowledge and fun.

What Not to Do:

Don't put the computer in your child's room or in an isolated part of the house if it can be avoided (exceptions include lap top models or computers used for business or by an older adolescent).

Don't forewarn your child about visiting unacceptable sites. It is better to react strongly and effectively if you learn this is happening.

Don't allow visits to Chat Rooms or Instant Messaging during childhood or early adolescence as these can led to situations that are anxiety producing or even dangerous.

What to Do:

Become watchful if your child seems to shut off the computer or switch sites when you enter the room or pass by.

Keep abreast of new computer developments and share these with your child. It can be a wonderful way of being close and encouraging competence.

As your child uses the computer for school, fun or general interest, take the opportunity to sit, and observe, and be available for questions and comments.

CRUELTY TO ANIMALS

Discussion:

If cruelty to animals occurs more than once or twice, it usually indicates that a significant psychological difficulty may exist.

It is more serious if a child is cruel to animals while alone rather than with a group of peers.

It is more serious if it involves a family pet.

Since a child's maturity doesn't allow for a full differentiation of animal feelings versus human feelings, cruelty to animals may be understood as an attempt to affect an animal as it would a human. This is why response should be full and effective.

A child's treatment of animals generally is modeled closely after parents' behavior toward other people and animals.

What Not to Do:

Don't assume that all abusive behavior is cruel. It may be normal curiosity when your child tests limits with an animal.

Don't call your child "cruel." Rather denounce the behavior.

Don't stress the animal's possible reaction to your child's behavior (i.e., a bite), but rather, the pain or discomfort suffered by the animal.

Don't restrict your child's contact with the animal after the incident.

What to Do:

Respond to your child's behavior in the presence of the animal.

As soon after the incident as possible, demonstrate to your child the proper way to handle and treat the animal.

For a while after the incident, emphasize "animal stories" when reading to your child.

Seek professional mental health consultation if the behavior cannot be controlled, if your child seems oblivious to the animal's distress, or if the cruel behavior is in any way bizarre or ritualistic.

DATING AND ROMANCE
Boys

Discussion:

There is romantic involvement when a boy has a significant relationship with a "girl friend."

For boys under age 16-17, there should not be the need for romantic involvement. What a boy that age does need is an evolving sense that he is competent, strong, and potentially attractive to girls.

Too much romantic involvement (repeatedly and constantly having a girl friend, or having a single, intense relationship with a girl) can be a danger sign.

The boy who always has a girl friend is likely to feel insecure about his competence and strength.

The boy who has an ongoing, intense relationship with a girl likely feels a need for care and is looking for it in this sort of relationship.

What Not to Do:

Don't bring attention to the fact that the boy has a girl friend by either teasing your child about it or by encouraging it.

Don't tell frequent stories about the boy friends or girl friends that you used to have. Your child wants to avoid this comparison or competition with you.

Don't think that by "breaking up" or interfering with the romantic relationship, you will be solving any underlying difficulties.

Don't be fooled into thinking that "romantic success" as a child will lead to similar success as an adult.

What to Do:

When your child starts to make reference to a "girl friend," simply acknowledge the statement, no more.

If you realize that the romantic involvement is taking too much time or energy or is causing obvious distress, that is your cue to exercise some control of the situation. Simply say that a particular behavior or activity is "not necessary," rather than saying your child is "too young" or could "get into trouble."

DATING AND ROMANCE
Girls

Discussion:

There is romantic involvement when a girl has a significant relationship with a "boy friend."

Girls under age 16-17 should not need an actual romantic involvement. However, girls this age do need romantic involvement in fantasy or in shared conversations with other girls.

Too much romantic involvement (repeatedly and constantly having a boy friend or having a single, intense relationship with a boy) can be a danger sign.

The girl who is too strongly romantically involved is usually showing a need for care and is attempting to get it from a boy.

What Not to Do:

Don't bring attention to the existence of a boy friend by either teasing your child about it or by encouraging it.

Don't tell frequent stories about the boy friends or girl friends that you used to have. Your child wants to avoid this comparison or competition with you.

Don't think that by "breaking up" or interfering with the romantic relationship, you will be solving any underlying difficulties.

Don't be fooled into thinking that "romantic success" as a child will lead to similar success as an adult.

What to Do:

When your child starts to make reference to a "boy friend," simply acknowledge the statement, no more.

If you realize that the romantic involvement is taking too

much time or energy or is causing obvious distress, that is your cue to take action. Simply say that a particular behavior or activity with the boy is "not necessary," rather than saying your child is "too young" or could "get into trouble."

DEATH QUESTIONS

Discussion:

A child who asks about death is really asking about care and security.

The idea of ceasing to exist is difficult for the child to grasp, but the idea of losing care if the parents cease to exist can very easily cause intense anxiety (fear).

In asking about death, the child is really asking for reassurance about parents' permanence and availability for purposes of care.

Death questions are a normal phase of development – a need to know about something that is vaguely threatening or unknown – and the proper responses quickly and effectively limit them.

Consultation with a mental health professional may be necessary when death questions become persistent and are causing the child significant discomfort.

There is a proper **way** to answer death questions rather than a specific proper **answer.**

What Not to Do:

Don't put your child off or minimize the importance of the questions.

Don't try to reassure your child. Your response should be direct, factual, and as unemotional as possible.

Don't make reference to relatives, pets, or others who have died who are known by your child, unless your child is asking specifically about them. Thus you avoid making the sense of loss part of the discussion.

Don't ask if your child is frightened of death. If fear is there, your questions won't make it go away. If there is no fear, your questions will raise the possibility that there should be.

Don't give answers that include descriptions or references to decay, to the body falling apart, or to being destroyed.

What to Do:

Whatever your explanation of death, whether it be consistent with your religious beliefs, or an original presentation of your own making, be sure that it is short, casual, simple. Use a description that your child already associates with positive feelings ("The angels carry you to heaven"; "You fall into a peaceful sleep forever"; etc.).

Persistent questions that seem associated with anxiety or depression, and that don't go away with the proper responses, may indicate a more generalized condition of emotional distress that may need professional evaluation.

DESTRUCTIVE BEHAVIOR
Ages 2–4

Discussion:

Destructive behavior is usually not based on any "desire to be destructive."

It usually results from the child's wanting to experience a sensation (tearing paper, fingers into the cake) or discover the effects of objects on each other (crayon on the wall, toy car against furniture).

Once the child has been told that the behavior is not acceptable, then persistent destructiveness may represent a test of the parents' response and the child's power.

It is easier to take such behavior if it is perceived as a normal aspect of development in this age group.

What Not to Do:

Don't spank as a first response.

Don't ignore the behavior if your child gives any indication of knowing it's not approved or "bad."

Don't label your child as "bad" but demonstrate that the behavior is unacceptable.

What to Do:

Tell your child firmly and directly (face-to-face) that the behavior or activity is not allowed.

As an optional next step (depending on your child's understanding and your patience) tell or show your child why the behavior or activity is not allowed.

Then either assume that your child will not repeat the behavior or remove the offending objects until the child reaches greater maturity.

DESTRUCTIVE BEHAVIOR
Ages 5-11

Discussion:

Destructive behavior among this age group often occurs with peers or follows peer examples.

Usually the child knows to some degree that it is wrong.

The behavior can be a reflection of stage-related psychological conflict, especially if persistent, occurring mostly with a particular parent, or following some type of pattern.

It may reflect healthy curiosity (taking things apart, using mother's makeup, trying to cook, etc.).

What Not to Do:

Don't label your child as "bad," just show disapproval of your child's behavior.

Don't ignore behavior of which your child knows you are aware.

Don't correct your child in front of peers, if possible.

Don't permit a situation where it is only one parent who assumes the role of "corrector."

Don't restrict your child from the destructive materials or situation, if possible. This would convey the message that you think the behavior will be repeated.

Don't keep bringing up previous destructive behavior when it is not the actual issue.

What to Do:

Speak with your child about the behavior, why he or she did it, and what might be the effects or consequences of the behavior.

Allow your child to make an apology. This will provide the child an important opportunity to save self-respect.

Communicate clearly any anger or disappointment that you feel as soon as possible.

Convey to your child that you have the power and determination to make sure the behavior doesn't occur again.

Obtain mental health consultation if the frequency or type of destructive behavior increases, or if there is a pattern that you can't interrupt.

DESTRUCTIVE BEHAVIOR
Adolescents

Discussion:

A child in this age range is more capable of serious destruction or destructiveness than are younger children, by virtue of strength, intelligence, and selective ability.

Patterns of destructiveness (repetitive) usually indicate real cause for concern about the child's development and/or stability. This is true whether the behavior is group-related or individual.

Occasional or random destructive behavior may only be reflecting the rapid mood swings or tendency to regress during these years.

This behavior demands quick and adequate response, as the child is capable of judging what has been done and needs some support.

What Not to Do:

If possible, don't respond only on the basis of the extent or type of destructiveness, but also find out what is your child's perception of the destructiveness.

Don't assume that your child has lost usual controls.

If there is not a definite pattern of destructiveness, don't automatically restrict or limit your child from the situation in which the destructiveness has occurred.

Don't forget that your child probably feels ashamed and unhappy about what has happened, even without your involvement.

Don't ignore destructive behavior, especially if your child is giving out signals about it.

Don't overuse remarks about how your child acted imma-
turely. This is a sore spot for most adolescents, since they are
all too aware that their behavior is often immature.

What to Do:

Clearly indicate to your child your anger, disappointment,
and surprise.

Encourage your child to describe what happened, in terms of
his or her feelings at the time, circumstances that occurred,
etc.

If you feel consequences are necessary, make them as
immediate and clear-cut as possible, and allow your child to
express feelings about them.

Allow as much privacy as possible from siblings and peers to
discuss the behavior, your feelings about it, and the consequences.

Seek professional mental health consultation if the destructive behavior becomes repetitive, more frequent, or in any
way endangers the health or life of your child.

DISCIPLINE, PUNISHMENT, AND RESISTANCE TO THEM

Discussion:

The major function of parents is to give care. The child looks to the parents for their ability to teach (about safety, about right and wrong) and to control in addition to care-giving.

Discipline is a combination of teaching and controlling, both in the interest of the child's care and security.

Discipline is not effective when the child continues to be bad and/or gets worse.

Effective discipline depends on the parents' ability to make the child afraid of their displeasure – afraid of losing their love. Therefore, parents have to communicate their displeasure effectively.

The child wants the parents to be good disciplinarians, and does not want to resist punishment.

What Not to Do:

Don't continue with discipline that doesn't seem to be effective, that is, which doesn't stop the behavior. This will only make your child angry and insecure. He or she will repeat the bad behavior or intensify it, unconsciously, to test whether or not you will discipline more effectively next time.

Don't punish your child by taking away objects or activities. This tactic may seem to work in the short term, but, ultimately, it fails because your child can adapt to the loss of anything (except your love). Your child will also realize that you don't have enough emotional power to force good behavior with just the strength of your words.

Don't give your child the message that you expect bad behavior.

Don't refer back to the bad behavior once the situation has been corrected.

Don't overlook or ignore bad behavior. If your child knows that you know about it but don't effectively control it, then the sequence of anger, insecurity, and the need to test your control and care will result in a repetition or progression of bad behavior.

Don't expect that anyone else can punish your child as effectively as you, the parent, can.

What to Do:

Identify for your child, clearly, what it is that you feel is bad or unacceptable behavior. Do this in the simplest way possible, with a minimum of words, with eye contact, and as soon as possible.

Within reason, use whatever means necessary to stop the behavior at the moment. Get an acknowledgment or promise from your child for the future. There is an order to what is "necessary." The most desirable parental response is a look of anger or displeasure. Next in order of preference would come, one by one, more and more intense responses: raising your voice, taking the child firmly by the arms or shoulders, and, as a last resort, spanking.

Once again, make the punishment immediate, emotional, and effective.

DRESSING AND GROOMING
Adolescents

Discussion:

Adolescents are especially concerned with their image. It is the way they judge their peers and are judged themselves, and it is the simplest way of belonging, or keeping apart.

In healthy development, there is a good balance between developing an individual look and still sharing a group image. In addition, the child has to deal with the need to develop antonomy – an individual identity – while still respecting family standards.

As a rule, the purpose of an adolescent's image is as a label, identifying the group (jock, burnout, preppy, deadhead, fag, etc.). A quick identification without any more significant information is just what an adolescent prefers.

Therefore, if a child's dress or grooming starts to change, there is a good chance that a significant emotional change is occurring as well.

As the adolescent is not widely experienced in subtle expression, dress or grooming may also not be subtle. Hence, the use of too much makeup, extreme hair styles, peculiar or rigidly styled dress, poor hygiene, etc.

What Not to Do:

Though your adolescent may seem grown up with regard to choosing and using clothing and other aspects of grooming, don't give up your role of remaining in charge.

Don't ignore or be too permissive about your child's dress or grooming. It can easily become an unconscious testing issue for your child, with the usual progression of insecurity, anger, and a further need to test you.

When you feel the need to intervene and control dress or grooming, don't label what is unacceptable as "bad," "too revealing," looking like a "bum or tramp," etc. Rather, firmly state in simple terms that the dress or grooming is unacceptable and must be changed.

Don't be taken in by the statement that "Everyone else dresses like this," "Everyone wears their hair this way," or "Other mothers don't care," etc. This may, in fact, be true for the group with which your child is trying to identify. It's the very reason you want to interrupt this identification.

What to Do:

Play an active role in helping your child buy or put together clothes. Although it is not always acknowledged, your approval and guidance is always appreciated.

If your child starts to develop or get into a new style or image that makes him or her uncomfortable, there will be signals sent out ("What do you think, Mom?"; "Do you think that girl's hair looks strange?"; "I don't like anything you pick out for me!"; etc.). You must help your child by being clear about your opinion and about the fact that you are in control.

DRUG USE: POT SMOKING, ETC.

Discussion:

As with certain other adolescent activities, peer pressure can be a major factor in whether or not and with what frequency the child uses drugs.

Drug use is of more serious concern if it occurs when the child is alone than if the child is in a group.

As with some other adolescent behavior, the child will indicate discomfort and wish to be controlled by dropping "hints" of drug use.

Aside from pure social peer pressure, drug use can represent the child's effort to escape from stress (real or perceived).

Legal restrictions and consequences make handling this type of behavior difficult and tricky.

The fact that money is necessary to acquire drugs and that drug use can impair major areas of functioning usually means that consequences of drug use can be far-reaching.

Controversial public data about the effects of drugs and the prevalence of drug use in adult society further complicate the handling of this behavior.

What Not to Do:

Don't ignore the "hints" that your child drops.

Don't be sneaky in your efforts to collect evidence of drug use. Be direct in your suspicions, accusations, searches, etc.

Don't confront or discipline your child in front of peers.

Don't stress the legal consequences and disapproval of society (although these certainly need to be mentioned). Rather, stress your own concern for your child and point out consequences in the child's functioning or comfort that are already obvious.

If possible, don't let your embarrassment or shame within the community affect the way you deal with your child.

Don't rely on separating your child from undesirable peers as a sure solution. It may be part of the solution, however.

What to Do:

Keep the discussions with your child as calm as possible, stressing your level of concern, and stating your knowledge of your child's discomfort.

Tell your child that you know you can't "force" a stop to drug use, that it has to come from the child, but that you are willing to apply whatever measures seem necessary to help stop it. This appears to be a contradictory approach, but it can be an effective one.

Attend to stresses of which you become aware in your child's life and environment.

Learn as much as you can about alcohol, marijuana, cocaine, prescription pills, and other drugs. Acquire literature, attend seminars. Seek professional chemical dependency consultation if the pattern of drug use becomes uncontrollable, if it escalates, if the child's emotional health is deteriorating, or if major areas of functioning become seriously impaired.

EATING PROBLEMS
Ages 3-11

Discussion:

Problems with eating are of concern only if they are persistent or interfere with health.

Many children go through stages where certain foods are disliked or refused.

At certain periods, eating with the family can be a stress and therefore, can affect eating behavior.

Subtle anger or frustration on the part of the parent(s) can have a great impact on the child in conjunction with food or eating issues.

What Not to Do:

Try not to make mealtime a battle or test of wills.

Don't link eating behavior with other issues, such as "being bad," "being unappreciative," etc.

Don't warn your child about poor eating behavior before it actually becomes evident at each meal.

Don't send your child away from the table, and thus, from the family.

Don't let your child's expressed tastes dictate what the rest of the family eats.

What to Do:

Let you child know clearly that you are aware of the eating difficulties.

At those times when you are going to serve something your child especially likes, point out that everyone likes it, so it will not be interpreted as special treatment for the one who has eating problems.

As much as possible, ignore signs of your child's difficulty, such as the taking of tiny portions, drinking to enable swallowing, and sad or disgusted facial expressions.

Strongly enforce the principle that there will be no snacking or dessert until the next meal if this meal isn't eaten.

EATING PROBLEMS
Adolescents

Discussion:

Eating problems are harder to define at this age, since individual food preferences, social activities, schedules, and self-imposed "diets" all interfere with normal eating patterns.

Cause for concern exists when there is visible or medically established evidence of malnutrition or excessive weight gain or loss.

These conditions are more usually representative of internal psychological difficulties rather than circumstantial factors.

What Not to Do:

Don't allow most of your child's dieting or eating to be done apart from the family.

Try not to make eating situations "power struggles."

Don't ignore "evidence" of possible eating disturbance, such as the child's eating a predominance of one type of food, rapid depletion of sweets or "junk foods" from around the house, frequent need for clothing of a different size, unwillingness to wear certain clothes or types of clothes.

What to Do:

Make your child aware of your suspicions or beliefs about the eating problem.

Without showing anger, let your child know that you expect him or her to continue engaging in the usual family eating habits and routines.

Let your child know you are aware that appetite, good food selection, and eating can all be related to one's emotional state.

Seek professional mental health consultation if a pattern of disordered eating becomes persistent.

FAVORITE ADULTS, OTHER THAN PARENTS

Discussion:

The term "favorite adult" could be applied to a neighbor, aunt, or other "preferred" adult with whom your child has a relationship.

It is important to realize that the preference is apparent and not actual. In fact, at the deepest levels, parents are always preferred.

Temporary or occasional preferences can be a reflection of quite normal development – a 13-year-old girl wanting to be around her attractive young aunt; a 12-year-old boy wanting to be in the company of his sports-oriented grandfather.

Of concern are patterns of preference that remove the child frequently, or much of the time, from the home and family, or that are inherently unsafe or damaging.

If such a pattern exists, it may reflect the child's attempts to have needs met in a better way than the parents are meeting them.

What Not to Do:

Don't let your own feelings of competition, anger, jealousy, or confusion be obvious to your child.

Don't prohibit the "preferred" relationship, unless it represents significant separation or is inherently unsafe or damaging.

Don't involve the "preferred" person in efforts to have your child give up the relationship, as this approach can easily backfire.

What to Do:

In a casual way, find out from your child what it is in the

"preferred" relationship that is pleasurable (what your child thinks of the person, what they do together).

Make your child aware that you realize what it is in the relationship that makes it pleasurable. In a subtle way, this makes you more a part of it.

Make changes in aspects of your own relationship so that it will better meet your child's needs.

If you make the decision that the "preferred" relationship should be curtailed (or terminated), say that you want your child to be at home more and with you more, because you like his or her company.

"FAVORITE" PARENT

Discussion:

There are times during a child's early and adolescent years when there clearly seems to be a preference for mother or father – to be with, to communicate with, or to model after that parent.

In the majority of situations, this preference is grounded on the developmental stage taking place at that time.

Sometimes, however, it is due to specific and powerful circumstances or messages having to do with, or coming from, one or both parents.

An apparent preference for one parent does not necessarily mean that the other parent is no longer loved or has done something wrong.

What Not to Do:

If possible, don't let you child know about any angry or hurt feelings that you, as the non-preferred parent, may be experiencing.

Don't encourage the preference, even if it feels good to be the preferred parent.

Don't focus on the preference by talking about it or making reference to it. This can interfere with your child's developmental needs.

However, don't ignore or accept a parental preference which results in rudeness, impoliteness, or other unacceptable behavior toward the non-preferred parent.

What to Do:

If the preference seems to cause high levels of discomfort for your child or you, the parents, or if it seems to cause your child's behavior to become difficult or unacceptable, then professional mental health consultation may be necessary, so that you will understand the basis for the preference and can use specific response and management techniques to deal with it.

FEAR, GENERAL DISCUSSION
Ages 4-9

Discussion:

Fear, in this discussion, is behavior in which the child demonstrates intense and/or inappropriate fear of a situation, person, or animal.

This difficulty can represent a normal stage of development, or it can signal a state of conflict that should have professional attention.

Parental response to this behavior can significantly enhance or damage the parent/child relationship.

If the fear is of a situation (or animal or person) that the child encounters commonly, then other areas of the child's functioning can be affected as well.

Fortunately, the child is very clear about the fact that he or she is fearful; parents will not have to guess what the problem is. Neither is it the type of difficulty that can be overlooked easily.

The child will usually have one predominant fear. If there are many fears, the situation may be serious, and the considerations in this chapter may not properly apply.

The fear may seem to occur more frequently in the presence of one parent rather than the other. Or, the child may turn to one parent more than the other while fearful. In either event, it should be that parent, primarily, who deals with the behavior.

What Not to Do:

Don't decide that there is significant difficulty until there have been several instances of the fear.

Don't try to help your child avoid the situation (or animal or person) that is causing the fear. To do so would reinforce your child's feeling that the fear is valid and that it affects you as well.

Don't offer your child a lot of reassurance. Again, that could cause your child to conclude that there is, indeed, a reason to be fearful.

Don't try to shame your child into "facing up" to the situation that is causing the fear.

Don't respond with anger to your child's fear.

What to Do:

Verbalize repeatedly to your child that you are aware of the fear and that you understand how upsetting it is to be fearful.

Tell your child that someday the fear will be gone.

Encourage your child to draw pictures, act out, or otherwise imitate the situation that is causing the fear.

"Forget" that your child is fearful; that is, expose your child to the situation, animal, or person if it is necessary or appropriate to do so.

Seek professional mental health consultation if the behavior doesn't improve or disappear over time, or if other areas of your child's functioning or comfort become affected.

FEAR OF THE DARK

Discussion:

An important aspect of a child's security at any moment is the ability to process and be comfortable with the environment. Darkness deprives a child of the ability to see the environment and who or what is in it.

An important developmental task for a child is defining reality. Darkness allows real and unreal to be confused. Therefore, fear of the dark is a common and understandable fear in children.

Whether this fear is a new one or one that has been present for some time, the parents will be expected to be, and should be, involved in helping the child to deal with it.

The peak ages for this fear are from age 3 to 9 or 10, but it can even be present in adolescents (who are better at hiding it).

Fear of the dark may take the form of a child refusing to stay in a dark room, or refusing to enter a dark room.

What Not to Do:

Don't spend time reassuring your child by using logical arguments or by putting on the light to show that there is "nothing really there."

Don't ridicule or call your child a "baby."

Don't force your child to stay in, or go into, a dark room.

Don't think that your child is afraid of nothing. Although not able to tell you the actual cause of the fear, the child's mind is likely conjuring images of a scary person or monster of some sort.

What to Do:

Let your child know that you are listening and that it must be very difficult to have that kind of fear.

Use a night light in your child's room, saying it is to help the child feel better, not that it will help him or her see there is nothing there to be afraid of.

Be willing to accompany your child into, or through, a dark room, only if you can make it seem like a natural thing to do. Do not make it a type of reassurance.

For a younger child who may verbalize fear of a "monster," suggest that the child draw it for you and encourage the child to include all the scary features in the drawing.

FEAR OF DIVORCE

Discussion:

For a child of any age the possibility of losing the security of the home and family can be very frightening.

Especially in times when divorce is commonly referred to in one way or another, it is a term which comes to represent a loss of security.

Fortunately, children have a healthy way of not paying close attention to things if they are not directly affected by them. Therefore, although divorce may be associated with a general sense of insecurity, real divorce fear doesn't occur unless the child's own parents seem to be involved.

Even with a lot of arguing between parents the child will not have a true fear of divorce, unless that word has been used by the parents during the arguing.

Of the many kinds of fears divorce fears are particularly difficult for the child, because the parents who are available to reassure about other types of fears can be too involved, themselves, in the marital situation to be of much help.

What Not to Do:

Don't assume that all questions about divorce truly represent fear or anxiety. They can be meant to elicit a general reassurance. The same applies to casual remarks or reports about friends' parents getting divorced.

Don't give your child excessive reassurances. As with other fears, this can backfire; you may leave your child even more uncertain.

Don't mention divorce or discuss the word "divorce" (if you are, indeed, going to go through one) until a decision is made.

What to Do:

When the decision has been made to divorce, supply the facts necessary for your childs' reassurance: which parent will be leaving, where the child will be living, how often visits will be made with the parent living away, and when these will take place.

Do let the child know they are not at fault.

No matter in what context your child presents fear of (your) divorce, let him or her know that you realize how upsetting an idea like that can be. Keep doing this.

Keep your discussions about your divorce as private as possible.

FEAR OF LOSING PARENTS

Discussion:

The actual fear is not of losing parents, but of losing the care parents provide.

The fear that the child usually verbalizes is that the parents may die, get sick, or be killed.

It is a fear that can appear if something has, in fact, happened to one parent or both parents or the child has become aware of another child losing a parent. These cases are rare, however. Occasionally, television material also prompts this fear.

Most often, fear of losing parents is an irrational fear that arises during a particular developmental stage or as a result of a difficult relationship between parent and child resulting in anger on the child's part.

This can appear to be a serious problem, because the child can scream or cry, resist being separated from the parents and cause trouble for the persons taking care of the child (grandparents, sitters, teachers, etc.).

What Not to Do:

Don't try to reassure the child by reasoning or using logic. This can serve to make the fear worse. If there is no logical basis for the fear, using logic does not work.

Don't let the child's fear cause you to change your plans, stay with the child, or contact the child while you are away.

Don't ridicule your child for the fear.

Don't make reference to the fear before it appears.

What to Do:

Acknowledge that your child has this fear and that it must be very uncomfortable.

Firmly control the expressions of this fear if they take the form of crying, screaming, physically acting up, or inappropriate behavior.

If these responses don't eliminate or effectively reduce the fear, appropriate mental health consultation may be necessary.

FEAR OF SCHOOL
Ages 5-10

Discussion:

It can be a fear involving any area or activity that would take the child away from home (not just school).

Fear of school is usually not caused by an actual school situation, although the school's handling of it can make it worse.

The fear often reflects conflicts between child and parent — mother, especially.

The child often uses illness or "pains" as a reason for not going to school.

It gets harder to deal with this problem the longer it goes on. Often, professional mental health consultation is necessary if early parental efforts don't work.

What Not to Do:

Don't let your child decide whether or not to go to school.

Don't accuse your child of "faking."

Don't pick your child up at school, unless the nurse reports actual evidence of illness.

Don't delay for long a consultation with a physician or pediatrician to rule out real physical illness.

What to Do:

Acknowledge your child's feelings of illness, but make it clear that school will be attended.

If the child refuses to go, within reason, take any measures necessary to get your child to school.

Try to determine areas of conflict. If you cannot and your child somehow succeeds in staying home frequently or repetitively, seek professional mental health consultation.

FEAR OF SCHOOL
Ages 11-17

Discussion:

In this age group, fear of school can be expressed as unwillingness to go to school, oversleeping, truancy, or "illness" (aches or pains).

If it is truly a persistent situation or a progressive pattern of behavior, seek professional mental health consultation promptly. In this age range this is usually a more difficult condition to correct without such help.

Fear of school can represent not only conflicts concerning parent(s) but also issues of socialization, peer pressure, or self-image.

What Not to Do:

Don't give your child the impression that occasional absences without good cause are "okay."

Don't threaten your child with punishment or consequences.

Don't feel you can coerce your child to school the way you would a younger child with this difficulty.

What to Do:

Try to find out (preferably from your child) about any circumstantial or personal stresses that are occurring.

Let your child know early that you regard this condition seriously and might seek professional consultation for it.

Contact the school to exchange with them ideas and information about the situation.

FEMININE BEHAVIOR
Boys

Discussion:

Feminine behavior involving speech, body movement, dress and grooming, and social and recreational interests does not necessarily have implications about sexuality or sexual preference.

Such behavior develops as a boy tries to get care and attention by identifying with, or attempting to please, a particular parent. The inclination toward feminine behavior develops slowly over a long time and in response to many subtle but consistent bits of feedback from that parent.

If this behavior is present in boys under age 11, there is good chance the boy can become more typically masculine as he passes through adolescence. If, however, the behavior is present throughout adolescence, it could remain throughout the boy's adult life.

Changing this behavior requires a knowledge of the interpersonal dynamics taking place and intelligent use of limitation and disapproval.

What Not to Do:

When you first realize there is a behavior that you feel is too "feminine," don't call your son a "sissy," "baby," etc.

Don't react in any extreme ways, if possible. Try to become aware of your own anxiety and control it. It is being stirred up by the undesirable behavior, making you uncomfortable and angry.

Don't get caught in the trap of mother encouraging some of this behavior while father gets angry about it, or vice versa.

What to Do:

Pick out a particular behavior (or speech, dress, etc.), and consistently and firmly tell your son that you don't like it. Don't give any further explanation, and don't throw in any implications about sexuality.

Feminine behavior may be too complex a problem for parents to change or influence without close professional mental health assistance.

FIGHTING
Boys, Ages 10-15

Discussion:

For boys this age, efforts to determine how their bodies function and how strong they are influences much of their social interaction.

The assessment of this functioning and strength has to be on a comparative basis. Therefore, rough play, mock combat, wrestling, etc., is not unusual and serves an important developmental purpose.

However, since there is a great sensitivity to the issue of strength (or weakness), it may not take much provocation for anger to appear if one boy makes another boy feel insecure physically.

Also, anger arising in other circumstances is likely to be expressed physically if words don't seem to be enough to "win."

Girls tend to become involved in physical fights less frequently and more sporadically than boys. Typically, they find other ways to express anger toward one another.

What Not to Do:

Don't be too concerned that physical fighting will do significant physical harm. Although boys this age might act or talk "tough," they still are very sensitive to bodily harm. Therefore, they will tend to control the amount of damage they do to each other.

Don't be surprised if boys who are fighting one day are friendly the next day.

Don't let a fight continue if you have the opportunity to intervene. Both boys will be grateful – although they won't necessarily show it – for the interruption.

What to Do:

If your child is often involved in fights, this is a danger sign. If he is the one who is starting the fights (the "bully"), this means that he is angry, insecure, and testing your ability to be in control. If he is the one who is picked on, this means that his peers are discerning some weakness or vulnerability in him which makes them uncomfortable and angry and, thus, likely to start a fight with your child.

The picked-on child needs your care. Show him that you know how hard it must be to be picked on. Avoid either too much sympathy or pushing him to be tougher. At the same time talk with him about the effective use of such techniques as maintaining eye contact. Help your child work on his self-confidence so he portrays a self-confident rather than a victimized stance. Be sure to help your child recognize when he can use help from authorities and encourage him to get it.

Control the fighting behavior as you would any bad behavior – quickly, intensely and directly. Showing that you care and are in control will reduce the anger, the insecurity, and the need to test.

FRIENDS, POOR CHOICES

Discussion:

To a small degree, your child's choice of friends is determined by where the child lives, the class at school, or which children are encourage by the parents to be together in play or socialization.

To a larger degree, however, choice of friends is determined by the behavior characteristics of those friends.

These behavior characteristics include how well-behaved the friends are, how well the friends achieve academically, how social the friends are, or what their level of athletic ability is.

A poor choice of friends exists when the characteristics of the friends are not what you think are appropriate for your child, or if the friends negatively affect your child's behavior.

Helping your child make a good selection of friends is one of the most important ways you can help current development, as well as future happiness.

What Not to Do:

Don't be concerned about an occasional poor choice of friend, if most of your child's friends are good choices.

If you have to comment about, or interrupt, a friendship that your child has made, don't indicate that you think your child would behave like the child of which you don't approve. Just say that you don't like your child to be around a child who is not behaving or acting properly.

Don't ignore your child's reports of bad behavior in friends. This is a common way for your child to test your response to bad behavior.

Don't let your child's needs for friends keep you from interrupting a bad friendship. Need for good care is more important.

What to Do:

When your child makes good choices in friends, encourage the friendships in whatever ways you can. Ask about the friends; suggest that they sleep over; invite them to join your family activities; speak specifically about what it is that you like about them.

Although it is true that you can't completely control your child's social contacts outside of the home, you can have a great influence on who your child picks as steady friends. First, comment about a poor choice of friends, then take appropriate control measures (firm, emotional disapproval, then clear demands that the friendship be ended).

HABITS

Discussion:

Habits are behaviors that are repetitive and serve no obvious purpose (thumb-sucking, nail-biting, face-picking, etc.).

They may appear relatively suddenly and last for a long time.

They may come and go and assume new forms, all related to each specific developmental stage of the child and to the stresses being experienced at that time.

The child's conscious awareness of a habit varies considerably.

What Not to Do:

Don't ridicule your child.

Don't try to stop the habit "by force." Since habits serve the purpose of attempting to reduce stress, they can't be stopped quickly.

Don't completely ignore the habit.

What to Do:

Start by calling your child's attention to the habit. Make your child aware that it is happening and that you are aware of it.

Alternate between firmly telling your child to stop and appearing to ignore the habit.

The balance between prohibiting and "ignoring" depends on how much the habit bothers you or is destructive to your child. This alternating approach will work, over time.

Consult a mental health professional if the habit progressively becomes more severe, if there are many habits, or if the relationship between you and your child is becoming strained as a result of the habit(s).

HELPLESSNESS
Under Age 10

Discussion:

A child is "helpless" when the child either is unwilling or unable to do things that he or she was formerly able to do, or is reluctant to learn new self-help skills.

If this behavior occurs in the absence of other functional or emotional difficulties, it is not serious.

This behavior usually represents a normal urge to regress temporarily.

However, even though this may be a "normal" behavioral difficulty, the response to it is still very important.

Not only will the child appear helpless, but the behavior will be coupled with the desire to enlist the presence or attention of the parents.

The behavior is often associated with circumstances that are stressful for the child: birth or "assertion" of a sibling, illness, parental absence, school, etc.

What Not to Do:

Don't lose sight of the temporary nature of this difficulty.

Don't refer to your child's behavior as immature or "babyish."

Don't refuse to offer some gesture of help, as requested.

If possible, don't respond to this behavior with anger, and certainly not with punishment.

What to Do:

Let your child know that you are aware how hard it must be to be unable to do something.

Remember at this age children can lose sight of specific tasks and become overwhelmed by the whole situation. Help your child to see the smaller steps.

Help your child to the degree that you feel comfortable.

Praise your child for those things obviously done well and capably.

If you are aware of some stress that exists, state that fact to your child.

HOBBIES

Discussion:

These are activities or efforts that typically involve a lot of time, the creation of something tangible but always a little out of reach, and the involvement of parents or other adults to some degree.

They provide a good way: to feel competent, to have something that feels good and is always available, to provide privacy, to provide structure, to compete safely, and to ask for adult assistance in a very defined way.

Hobbies are important developmental forms of play.

What Not to Do:

Don't go too far in suggesting or pushing hobbies – your child should be the one who decides what type of hobby and when to pursue it.

Don't "take over," or help too much with your child's hobby — it should be for his or her pleasure and development, not yours.

Don't feel you have to continue to support a hobby if it gets too expensive or requires too much space or time. State the facts to your child and suggest a modified or similar hobby.

Don't let your child use a hobby to become separated or isolated to an extreme.

What to Do:

Show interest in your child's hobby by asking about it, observing it, and occasionally mentioning your own ideas about it.

Show your support by making available what may be necessary for the hobby: a physical place or setup, your time, your money, and your assistance.

Show that you understand the seriousness and importance of the hobby by commenting about progress, growth, improvement, etc., that may be occurring and by mentioning it to other important adults (grandparents, neighbors, friends, etc.) while your child is present or can hear you.

Realize that hobbies may be given up or dropped quite suddenly, when they no longer provide positive developmental feelings for your child. Also recognize that hobbies are not developed for the sake of career potential (for example not all child athletes or artists need to become professional).

HOME AVOIDERS
Children

Discussion:

If all is going well in the parent/child relationship, the child will not consistently stay away from home for long periods.

A child needs to "touch base" regularly.

The occasional stay-away is probably due to very enjoyable play activity or welcoming home of a friend.

If your child is truly avoiding home, you should assume his or her needs are not being met adequately.

Home avoidance will get worse and worse unless its causes are corrected.

What Not to Do:

Don't allow your child to avoid home. Communicate clearly that you want your child with you or around the house ("You're so great!"; "I love being with you!").

Don't let a situation that may be easier for you (it can, after all, be less bother for you when your child is not around the house) lull you into the belief that your child is having a better time with friends than he or she would be having with you. The truth is, your child is missing you.

Don't let any anger that you feel about your child being away become a force to drive your child still further away.

What to Do:

If you become aware of a problem in your relationship with your child attend to it immediately, don't procrastinate.

Give clear messages about when you want your child home. If

the child is very young and stays away, go fetch your child after a reasonable time.

Keep sleep-overs relatively infrequent for children under age 10.

HOME AVOIDERS
Adolescents

Discussion:

Since adolescents have the means to travel far from home, socialization frequently takes place away from home. And since one important task of adolescents is to see whether parents can still control them and care for them, avoidance becomes a real possibility.

Avoidance is probably happening if parents suddenly realize that they are not seeing the child much or if the child seems to be making an issue of being away.

Boys and girls are equally likely to avoid home.

What Not to Do:

Don't ignore repetitive instances of home avoidance: missed curfews; your child not letting you know when he or she will be staying with a friend for a few hours; "walking the streets"; or "hanging around" outdoors.

Don't hesitate to ask about plans. Your child wants you to be "nosy." It shows you care.

What to Do:

Let your child know that you are not together as much as you would like and that you enjoy your child's company.

Insist that your child be home more. Be specific about when the child is to be home (eating dinner with you, spending more hours with you in the evenings and on weekends).

Make sure that you make some type of regular contact when your child is home (walking past and giving a pat on the shoulder, asking about what the child is doing, mentioning something that you've just been thinking or doing).

"HOMEBODY" CHILDREN

Discussion:

A "homebody" is a child who is rarely away from the home.

This situation is rarely a problem.

As a good home is the source of good care, children want to get as much as they can.

Since school and moderate social or sport activities provide sufficient exposure to the outside world for most children, the home is the appropriate place to relax, recharge, and regress.

What Not to Do:

Don't feel that your child is "missing out" if he or she is a homebody. Children expose themselves to life outside the home when they are ready to do it.

Don't "push" your child out of your house. Your feelings about what your child should experience may not be what the child is actually ready to experience.

What to Do:

Let your child know, in a way appropriate to the age, how much you enjoy and value being together.

Be receptive to your child's friends. The best way to help your child become comfortable socially is by using the security of home to promote outside-the-home friendships.

"HYPERACTIVE" BEHAVIOR
Young Children

Discussion:

While the description "hyperactive child" most often truly reflects the child's level and type of motor activity, occasionally it also reflects the parents' level of tolerance or patience, or their inability to effectively control the child's motor behavior.

The child's activity level at any stage is a result of the particular combination of curiosity and motor ability. High curiosity plus low motor ability equals low activity level. Low curiosity plus high motor ability equals low activity level. But high curiosity plus high motor ability equals "getting into everything."

There is a small percentage of children who are "hyperactive," based on an immaturity or developmental lag of the central nervous system. These children need careful pediatric evaluation and, perhaps, medication.

What Not to Do:

Don't refer to this behavior as "bad."

Don't allow your child to get into activities or areas that may not be safe. The best way to enforce these limits is to make dangerous or destructive objects unavailable by rearranging cupboards, using secure latches, etc.

Don't allow your child to get you into situations where you find yourself uncomfortable or angry. Take control; reduce the area of play by blocking off parts of a room or using a playpen.

Don't ignore (or try to ignore) an increasing activity level. Often your child is looking for you to provide some limitation or control and will intensify activity to get a response from you.

Don't separate your child from you (moving the playpen out of your view, sending your child outside to play a lot) because of the child's high level of activity. To do so could make your child feel naughty, and it will take him or her out of your area of control.

What to Do:

Make the experience of active play as positive and productive as possible by keeping your child comfortable and controlled, and by knowing that you are in control and able to enjoy your child's play.

JOKES AND HUMOR

Discussion:

The development of a sense of humor has important implications for your child. It can, and should, play a role in personal and social comfort and pleasure.

"Sick" jokes are a type of humor that has specific importance in both developmental and social contexts. The essence of this type of humor is to present the idea of illness, bodily harm, or victimization but with a traditional punch line or unexpected twist.

For a child who has fears of being hurt or victimized, or who is insecure, this kind of humor is an attempt to feel better by mastering those very fears.

For a child who has the need to feel competent or popular with friends, effective presentation of this type of humor is likely to get the desired feedback.

What Not to Do:

Don't encourage this type of humor by being receptive to it or by using such humor yourself. This kind of humor can have a subtle, threatening effect when used by adults or parents.

Don't forbid it, though, unless it seems to be occurring a lot or the subject material is in "bad taste" according to the family standards.

Don't laugh at your child's inappropriate joke-telling.

What to Do:

Comments need to be made about how the joke is not in good taste.

LYING
Ages 4-12

Discussion:

A child who knowingly doesn't tell the truth, is lying.

All children will lie to their parents at some point, as a test of their own power and as a test of parents' ability to "know" and be in control.

Lying can include evasions, distortions, or omissions as well as denials.

This behavior must be dealt with quickly, consistently, and effectively to ensure truthfulness in later years.

What Not to Do:

Don't ever ignore lying.

Don't shame or humiliate your child in dealing with it.

Don't refer to it, except at the time you are actually dealing with it.

What to Do:

Insist that your child admit to the lying and tell the truth, both at the time you are dealing with the lie.

Praise your child for telling the truth.

The consequences for lying as for any other misbehavior would be to show your angry, emotional disapproval.

Seek professional mental health consultation if you see a pattern of lying develop that you can't stop.

LYING
Adolescents

Discussion:

An adolescent is much more likely to lie if the child feels angry, resentful, fearful, or unfairly treated.

It is also much more likely to occur and continue if the child perceives the parent(s) as untruthful.

If not dealt with effectively (and quickly), lying can become a habitual way of dealing with the adult world.

If lying has not occurred regularly with the child in early years, parents can usually recognize "new" lying in adolescence quite quickly. This is because the adolescent is, at first, very personally uncomfortable with lying and will give out signals of that discomfort.

What Not to Do:

Don't apply punishment or consequences only. A full discussion of the lying incident is essential.

Don't force your child to "retract the lie and tell the truth." The child is very capable at this age of knowing the difference between truth and lie.

Don't tell your child that, as a result of the lie, you will become distrustful in other areas.

Don't shame (or expose) your child in front of peers or siblings. This might interfere with the child's ability to learn from the incident.

Don't refer to the lying incident in the future. Your child will want to believe it is forgotten.

What to Do:

State clearly to your child that you know how upsetting it

must have been to have lied and to have lived with the lie.

Let your child know that you are personally disappointed (perhaps angry) that the lying occurred.

Hold a lengthy, serious, and private discussion with your child, so that the "air is cleared."

Seek professional mental health consultation if a pattern of lying becomes evident and cannot be interrupted. An atmosphere of distrust breeds trouble for adolescents.

MESSINESS

Discussion:

"Messiness" is when a child makes (or leaves) things dirty, in disarray, or out of place.

The younger the child, the more likely it is that he or she will be messy (and the more it is part of normal development). The older the child, the less it should happen. If it happens a lot, it may represent poor teaching and follow-up by the parent, a period of regression or testing, or a sign of emotional distress.

A sense of neatness, order, and cleanliness is a valuable contribution parents can give for their child's future comfort and success.

What Not to Do:

Try not to interfere with your young child's pleasure or learning, for the sake of cleanliness or orderliness. If hands and face have to be cleaned up, do it after the eating, or after the playing outside is done. If toys need to be picked up, do it after the play is completed.

Don't make messiness the equivalent of being bad.

Don't let your child's messiness appear to be something that hurts you or makes you seem weak or vulnerable.

Don't let your adolescent remain messy. The longer it goes on, the angrier your child will become that you haven't corrected the behavior and the more difficult it will be to correct.

What to Do:

Your child will learn not to be messy by observing and following your example. Make cleanliness and neatness a part of your own living. Be an example by the way you give care and by the orderliness of the surroundings you provide.

For children of most ages — sometimes even for adolescents — it is often better to teach or help the child with the cleanup, than simply to demand it. Remember, the purpose of all this is really not to make your life easier, but to instill a way of living in your child.

Be lavish with your praise when your child has put things in order. The child has a need for this type of motivation.

MONEY
Children

Discussion:

Children derive their security from their parents. But since their parents derive a lot of their security from money, there is a potential problem for children when money is discussed.

Children assume that all of their security needs will be met, and they naturally expect many things to be provided: emotional love, food, shelter, playthings, money. Any limitation of these things will cause concern in your child.

Children think of money within the framework of their parents' messages about it. If the parents don't indicate otherwise, children assume there is enough money, just as they assume there is enough food.

Children aren't ready to learn the value of money until the age of 11 to 12.

The best way to produce a financially responsible adult is to raise an emotionally secure child.

What Not to Do:

Don't give money with "strings attached," as payment for a task performed, or as a reward for good behavior or performance.

Don't spend a lot of time talking to your child about how much things cost. Do this only when there is something that your child actually wants that costs too much. Even then, keep it short; just say it "costs too much."

Don't discuss family finances or your own financial concerns in front of your child.

Don't feel that giving your child money in a natural and free way will "spoil" his or her future appreciation of money.

What to Do:

Give your child money as you would food or a toy – naturally and appropriately to your standards.

Give your child an allowance if it is important to you. The benefits to both of you are a repetitive and consistent occasion for giving. Giving your young child money as needed, rather than as an allowance, is just fine also.

If you request that your child do a chore or task, make your appreciation and praise the reward, rather than money.

MONEY
Adolescents

Discussion:

Adolescents are still children, but they require money. They know what things cost. They often compete on the basis of money.

They think of how much money might be in their future.

They are likely to measure their parents' care on the basis of money. Accordingly, parents must make that care available in a controlled, consistent, and appropriate way.

This combination of factors makes the handling of money with adolescents potentially difficult.

What Not to Do:

Don't use money as a means of disciplining or controlling your child.

Don't regard making money available as an extra. In fact, your child expects money, as any other form of care.

If your child earns his or her own money, don't give up your right to monitor the way it is spent. Continue giving some money in addition to what the child earns.

Don't make an allowance contingent on behavior or other expectations. If your child falls down in these areas, discipline emotionally, not financially.

Don't mention the state of your finances in connection with how much money you give your child. Simple statements that something "costs too much" or that your child is "spending too much" are sufficient.

What to Do:

If you give an allowance, let your child spend it. Intervene only if there is a situation that you regard as inappropriate or not in keeping with family standards.

Freely ask if your child has enough money; offer some when the child is going out with friends. Knowing that your care is available in this form helps eliminate any connection in the child's mind between money and deprivation.

Remember that your child's sense of value — the value of money — will develop naturally in the child's dealings with the outside world.

MUSIC INVOLVEMENT

Discussion:

Except for touch sensation, auditory sensation is the earliest to develop effectively. It is an early means of receiving comfort and getting care. This is why music and songs are pleasurable for even young babies.

All through childhood and adolescence, music is a way to gain reassurance (by repetitive songs and jingles, by repeatedly listening to the "Top Ten Hits"). It is a way to be socially involved (singing in school and at camp, listening to and dancing to rock music). And it is a way to gain a sense of competence (playing musical instruments, singing in the choir, collecting large numbers of records and tapes).

What Not to Do:

Don't neglect any opportunity to expose your child to music. The more variety, the better.

Try not to limit or prohibit music in your house, unless it is a major disturbance or is inappropriate.

Don't feel that an apparent over-involvement with, or avoidance of, some types of music by your child is likely to be a permanent condition. It is most probably stage- and age-related.

What to Do:

Start early singing to, or with, your child. Make music in the house a common occurrence.

If your child likes or "is into" a particular type of music that you don't like, try to find something positive to say about it.

Whistling, singing, or humming on your part is an effective way of communicating to your child that you are emotionally comfortable.

Find ways to let your child be in charge of making or listening to music – from a record player and musical toys for your toddler, to a stereo system for your adolescent.

Encourage some type of formal music involvement for your child while he or she is growing up – whether it be school chorus, going to musical events with you, playing an instrument, or whatever.

PHONE BEHAVIOR
Age 11 and Over

Discussion:

Talking on the telephone is the best way for a child to communicate in private, secure surroundings and in the most anxiety-free manner possible.

In fact, using the telphone is such an important activity that the child may act as if the phone is his or her own exclusive property. He or she may lose all sense of time, become angry if interrupted, and allow telephone use to interfere with homework and other family activities.

What Not to Do:

Don't let phone use: take up too much time, keep other family members from using the phone, interfere with home-work or other responsibilities, cause your child to be isolated from the family for long stretches of time, or become too expensive.

Don't listen in on your child's phone conversations for more than the instant it may take to make sure the call has been picked up.

Don't tell your child's friends who call that your child is too busy to come to the phone, is eating dinner, etc. Let your child take that responsibility.

Don't get your child a private phone line. This can allow too much unmonitored time on the phone, or calls of which you are not aware. A phone extension in your child's room should be more than adequate.

What to Do:

Respect your child's privacy. Understand the need to make or receive phone calls in private.

Be diligent in passing along all phone messages.

Be firm in controlling phone "abuse." If necessary, set specific guidelines regarding phone use – what hours the phone will be available, maximum length of calls, etc.

Ask casually and briefly about who is calling. This lets your child know that you are aware of his or her phone use and are monitoring it.

PHYSICAL CONTACT AND TOUCHING

Discussion:

The sense of touch is the earliest sense to develop. It is operational at birth and, through it, the baby learns that parents exist and are there to give care.

The more parents touch the child and are in physical contact, the more they establish this very basic sense of closeness and care.

The child will continue to want physical contact with parents throughout life, even though there will be developmental stages where this doesn't seem to be the case. During these stages the nature of the physical contact should change according to the child's comfort.

Consistent and loving physical contact will enable the child to feel comfortable and will establish the ability to make physical contact with others.

What Not to Do:

Don't believe you can touch or hold your baby too much. The more the better!

Don't feel that your child is too old for appropriate physical contact. A child is never too old. Don't be put off if your child tells you that he or she is too old for physical contact during a time of anger or withdrawal. This may be a way of testing you.

Don't hesitate to interact physically with your child in the presence of friends. Even as an adolescent, your child still expects you to be consistent with your physical expression. In fact, your child's friends can have a positive experience when they witness parents giving physical affection.

What to Do:

Simply be free with your physical affection and touching and enjoy it! Giving this kind of care feels good to you as well as to your child.

PLAYING GAMES

Discussion:

Playing games is a wonderful way to be close to a child. As a family activity – and especially individually between one parent and one child – game playing provides for an exchange of pleasure and ideas, a sense of intelligence and skill, an experience of strength and competence, a manageable exposure to the parents' vulnerabilities.

There are stages in life and development where a child may seem to want to play games (or a particular game) excessively, or when the child may be resistant to game playing. In fact, both attitudes may seem to be present at the same time (as with a child who pushes to play a particular game, but at the same time, seems to develop anxiety while playing it).

Handling the game situation well can add a lot to the parents' pleasure and to the child's good development.

What Not to Do:

Don't push your child to play games, unless it is a family situation and you feel it is important that your child not feel excluded.

Don't win games a lot more than your child does. For a boy especially, a father winning a lot is the surest way to make a son resist playing games.

Don't continue with games that seem too difficult or complicated. This can interfere with the pleasure and sense of competence that game playing should provide.

Don't continue with games that seem to cause a deep distress. (Distress might appear as irritability, anxious giggling, or overactive physical behavior.)

What to Do:

Stay with the games that your child wants to play. A child knows best which ones give pleasure. The game is for your child; your own pleasure is a nice bonus, but it is not the main objective.

Until your child reaches age 15, make sure you let your child win most of the time. If you have to cheat, be sneaky, or even lie to do this, it is still best for your child's development. When you lose, keep smiling.

Be flexible about the rules of the game. Your child may make them up to meet the need to win and have fun.

PLAYING REPETITIVELY

Discussion:

Play is "fun" for children, because it serves basic developmental purposes.

The more developmentally important it is, the more any type of play is likely to be repetitive. Examples would be a 4-year-old boy who pushes toy cars around with loud noises (He is learning about power, strength, and motion); a 14-year-old boy shooting baskets for hours (He is learning athletic ability and competition); a 7-year-old girl whiling away an afternoon playing with her doll house (She is learning about care and modeling after her mother.).

What Not to Do:

The repetitive play may get on your nerves or may tax your patience, especially when your child insists on your participation. However, don't try to redirect your child's play.

Don't be surprised if play that has been repetitive suddenly disappears. That simply means it no longer provides developmental satisfaction.

Don't try to change the form, materials, or pace of your child's play. A child knows best what it should be.

Don't insist on joining in this play if your child seems to resist openly or if the level of enjoyment obviously decreases once you have joined in.

What to Do:

Give your child the idea that you appreciate the importance of play. Make comments that show you are interested, or take the time to observe.

PRACTICING AND PRACTICE BEHAVIOR

Discussion:

Informal practice takes place with children all the time. They practice riding their bikes, playing ball, playing games, driving the car, etc.

It is formal practice – the practice that is planned, regulated, and controlled by adults – that can cause difficulty within the parent/child relationship, as well as just for the child.

Whether it be musical practice, dance practice, or athletic practice, there is a balance to be maintained between the repetitive work of the activity that has to be mastered and the pleasurable feeling that comes with mastering it.

Unpleasant feelings associated with practice situations not only may interfere with a long-term involvement with the activity, but also may negatively influence the undertaking of other activities that require practice.

It is the parents' needs, expectations, or conflicts about the activity itself, or the very idea of practice, that will cause practice difficulty.

What Not to Do:

Don't make practice optional for your child. Sooner or later there will be an attempt to exercise that option to a degree that may not be compatible with effective practicing.

Don't make practice so rigid that your child feels an inability to resist, to rebel, or to procrastinate. Some flexibility is necessary for effective practicing within a healthy parent/child relationship.

Don't tell your child that the practice is for building character, for discipline, or even for future mastery of the activity. Instead, say that it is to help your child get better and better at the activity.

Don't use prolonged or reduced practice sessions as a punishment or reward. You can be flexible about length of practice sessions and should relate the length of any one session to how your child is performing generally or to your observation that your child has "done enough" for that day.

If your child resists or refuses to practice, don't introduce any other consequences (You can't play, can't watch TV, etc.) besides your emotional displeasure. That is what must be the controlling factor.

What to Do:

Have the practice time fit into the daily routine, as much as possible.

Refer to the practicing itself or to the practice time in a variety of ways: "It's time to work on that new song now."; "Let's see how you are doing with that new dance that you're learning."

Be free with your praise and share with your child your sense of his or her accomplishment.

Speak freely to others in front of your child about doing well, accomplishments, talent.

PRIVACY BEHAVIOR

Discussion:

This is behavior specifically for the purpose of limiting parents' access to, and awareness of, a particular activity. It is both socially and developmentally derived, and it serves the function of helping a child avoid anxiety.

It may take the form of a closed door, a lowered voice, or a command to "go away."

Beginning with toilet activities, this behavior progresses to body exposure, and then to sexual and social activities.

If handled correctly, this behavior will be specific and limited, and will make an important contribution to mutual respect.

What Not to Do:

Don't anticipate a need for privacy. Let your child express the need for it, unless behavior is occurring that seems inappropriate.

Don't make fun of your child's privacy behavior.

Don't purposely invade your child's privacy. If invasion of privacy occurs accidentally, make a simple, sincere apology. Nothing more is required.

Don't let appropriate privacy develop into separation or withdrawal behavior.

What to Do:

Let your child set the privacy guidelines.

Help enforce privacy needs between siblings. Brothers and sisters are not always as cooperative or respectful of one another as they should be.

PROMISCUOUS BEHAVIOR IN ADOLESCENTS

Discussion:

This is defined as sexual behavior that is excessive or inappropriate to family standards and morals.

This is a situation that usually develops over time; if it is a sudden, very uncharacteristic behavior it may indicate a serious emotional disturbance.

Although the behavior is sexual, the emotions causing it have more to do with the need for care and a feeling of competence.

If not dealt with effectively later adult heterosexual relationships can be adversely affected.

The child usually would like to stop this behavior.

Depending on their own adolescent sexuality, parents can have significant trouble responding to this type of behavior.

This behavior can affect functioning and comfort in all other major areas.

What Not to Do:

Don't ignore signals your child may send out: staying out late; being secretive or untrustworthy about the boys or girls that are dated; questions or comments about pregnancy, abortion, paternal responsibility, or birth control; association with girls or boys with a "fast reputation."

Don't give your child excessive messages about "being careful" or "not parking," etc. – by this age your child should be capable of knowing what situations to avoid – from your training and from peer knowledge.

Don't give your child threats about what would happen if a pregnancy occurs – this can backfire.

Don't equate your child's promiscuous behavior with "being bad," "being wild," or with "not being a good son or daughter."

Don't forget that even though this behavior seems very adult, your child remains very much a child in other ways.

What to Do:

Do all you can to reestablish closeness and communication with your child.

Verbalize in a general way your knowledge that girls sometimes feel the need to be close to someone, or that sexual interaction with a girl can make a boy feel more manly.

If your child in any way requests a physical, arrange it, and alert the physician or other health practitioner that the child may have questions about venereal disease, AIDS, pregnancy, intimacy, etc.

Seek professional mental health consultation to deal with those personal and family issues that may need attention.

PSEUDOMATURE BEHAVIOR

Discussion:

To some degree, judging a child to be mature is subjective, and based on what you consider to be normal behavior for the age.

If there is, in fact, behavior that is more mature than normal (pseudomature), your child has developed it in an attempt to remain comfortable when stressed.

Pseudomature behavior may not work to the child's best advantage, because it can lead adults to assume the child needs less care, when in fact he or she may actually need more care. Peers may feel uncomfortable being around a pseudomature child, thereby increasing stress further.

Although pseudomaturity may be the most obvious behavior, close examination will probably reveal immature behavior as well.

What Not to Do:

Don't make your child feel that this type of behavior is wrong. It won't be helpful and won't result in the behavior being dropped.

Don't encourage the behavior, believing that it truly represents advanced development.

What to Do:

Often pseudomature children are fearful of making mistakes. They need to know mistakes are normal.

Help the child to play freely if playing presents additional difficulty.

If you feel this behavior is causing your child difficulty, the best strategy is to call attention to the behavior in an interpretive way: "I notice you like to speak using big words"; "I see that you can be very polite to people." This makes your child realize that you know what is going on and also increases the child's own awareness of the behavior.

REGRESSIVE BEHAVIOR

Discussion:

Regression is taking place when the child seems to be acting or talking like a younger child.

Every child, at any age, can regress. It is a normal aspect of development and serves the purpose of allowing the child to regain comfort at a time of real or perceived stress.

The degree of regression is not measured by how young the child seems to act or talk, but rather by how long it continues.

The child is truly not completely aware of this behavior and does not consciously plan it.

The regressive behavior may be subtle and disguised, thereby allowing for a quiet regression (a 16-year-old adolescent who, after being very active socially, suddenly begins hanging around the house on Saturday nights); or it may be particularly obvious, demanding a response from you (a 6-year-old who suddenly can no longer get dressed alone).

What Not to Do:

Don't feel you need to immediately explore, address, or reverse this behavior. You may be interrupting something necessary for good development. Intervene only when the behavior persists for a long period (as a rule, more than a few weeks), is markedly inappropriate (an older child sucking a thumb in public), or is obviously causing your child distress (classmates making fun of your child for not wanting to take part in rough play for fear of being hurt).

Don't label the behavior "babyish." If you have to call attention to it, say your child is "acting younger than usual" or something else that actually describes what is taking place.

What to Do:

Once you become aware of this behavior, give your child some time to relinquish the behavior. Then if necessary, comment directly about what your child is doing. Become firmer and more intense, as needed, to interrupt the behavior.

If you are aware of stress operating on your child, attempt to alleviate it.

RELIGIOUS QUESTIONS OR INVOLVEMENT

Discussion:

Religious involvement is a wonderful way of getting and sharing care in the company of parents, friends, and others in the community.

Religion involves care; it encompasses issues of being bad and good; and it centers around God (the ultimate parent). Accordingly, it can play an important developmental role. However difficulties in development can appear in the context of religion or religious issues.

The general rule about "healthy" religious development is that, throughout childhood and most of adolescence, religious ideas and involvements should reflect those of the parents.

Therefore, the child who denies the religious involvement of the parents, or who becomes much more intensely involved with religion than the parents, is probably having a difficult developmental time.

The presence of questions about religious issues indicates normal developmental interest, except when those questions become intense (or constant), seem to be associated with anxiety, or defy the parents' attempts to answer them.

What Not to Do:

Don't feel that you have to provide the religiously accepted answers to your child's questions. Your child wants your answers, since the question probably has to do with issues associated with you.

Don't provide an answer to more than your child is asking. Keep the answers simple and short.

Don't worry about questions that seem to deny religion (or God) or seem to be defying religion (or God). These questions actually have more to do with you and your responses than they do with religion itself.

Don't allow your child to misbehave in activities associated with religion (your younger child acting up in Sunday school class; your adolescent not attending church with you, etc.).

Don't overlook the fact that many questions about religion are actually questions about you: your ideas about care, your strength of conviction, and your consistency.

What to Do:

Let your child know that questions about religion are as acceptable as any other kind of question.

If your child's questions seem to indicate too much involvement, or if they suggest some personal trouble, let your child know you are aware. These questions and involvements are important, and your child probably is not feeling comfortable.

If your child of any age challenges or denies the family's religious involvement, acknowledge what your child is saying, but also firmly require that he or she follow family traditions and behavior.

RESISTING BED OR BEDTIME
Young Children

Discussion:

Children, especially young children, like to be with their parents.

No matter how attractive their bedroom, no matter how comfortable the bed, no matter how pleasant the bedtime routine, there is an inevitable resistance to being separated from the parents.

Children can find all sorts of ways to postpone or interrupt their bedtime. They can keep coming back to the parents, asking the parents to come to them, asking for a drink, saying they are afraid of the dark.

It is important to manage this behavior in a firm enough way to get the child to bed consistently, and yet preserve bedtime as a time for closeness and care.

What Not to Do:

Once the bedtime routine is complete (stories, songs, prayers, hugs, or whatever else you like to do) don't allow more than one or two postponements, on an occasional basis. Don't even allow these one or two postponements, if they start to occur regularly.

Don't try to control the behavior by shutting your child's door or by putting up a gate.

Don't control the behavior by trying to reason or argue with your child.

Don't think that making the bedtime earlier or later will be a solution.

What to Do:

Firmly tell your child that you do not want to hear or see the child until the morning.

Escalate and intensify this message in whatever way necessary to get the desired results. A child who is reassured by your control will be able to enjoy a reasonable, comfortable bedtime.

RESPONSIBILITY DEVELOPMENT

Discussion:

When the child doesn't behave in a way parents expect, this represents irresponsible behavior.

Responsibility is taught. It is taught more easily if the child feels like a good child and thereby expects and wants to retain the parents' approval.

The basic motivation for the child to carry out responsibilities is parental approval. Accordingly, it is important to express that approval on a regular basis. This is why the idea of long-term responsibility (or "chores") is not a good one. Over time, the parent might forget to give the approval, and the child's risk of becoming "bad" (by neglecting or forgetting the responsibility) increases.

What Not to Do:

Don't give your child the idea that carrying out a particular responsibility is necessary for the welfare of the family, or especially for you, the parent. Your child will perform best (be most responsible) when perceiving the family situation to be secure and you to be strong.

When your child neglects a responsibility, be firm and limit your disapproval to what specifically has been neglected. Don't give a general message that your child is bad.

If possible, don't assign a number of responsibilities at the same time, and don't present or post a list. This tends to dilute the approval factor.

Try not to "order" your child to be responsible. It diminishes motivation for approval.

Don't compare your child's "responsibilities" to those of his or her siblings. This will interfere with the sibling relationship, and it violates the principle of keeping misbehavior issues between you and your child exclusively.

What to Do:

Be sure responsibilities considered for your child are appropriate and realistic.

As you assign a responsibility or refer to an area of responsibility, mention both your appreciation and your approval.

Give praise liberally for responsible behavior. An effective way to do this is to allow your child to "overhear" such praise when you are talking with friends or family in person or on the phone.

RISK-TAKING BEHAVIOR
Adolescents and Preadolescents

Discussion:

This is behavior that you know is dangerous and that your child knows is dangerous (However, don't expect your child to reveal the behavior or admit to it.).

It typically involves putting the body at risk (wild bike or skate board use, riding dirt bikes or motorcycles too fast and/or without a helmet, wild "show-off" behavior at the beach or amusement park).

In a less serious form, it is an expression of physical ability, competence, or strength for the benefit of peers (male or female). In this context, it has more of a social appearance and significance.

In its more serious form, it is a way of "flirting" with danger for the subconscious purpose of getting care. This behavior can appear in groups, but is also notorious for occurring when the child is alone.

Unfortunately, injury or pain resulting from the behavior does little to modify the more serious form.

What Not to Do:

Don't dismiss as "just a stage" or "just being a kid" behavior that truly seems dangerous. Typically, your child will let you know in some way about taking risks. For you not to respond definitively can be translated as not caring.

Don't spend too much time arguing or reasoning with your child about the behavior. Words can only go so far – and possibly, not far enough.

Don't try to control the behavior merely by restricting your child or eliminating the activity. Do that if necessary, but the ideal response is to make the child stop taking the risks. Showing you care this way eliminates the child's need to get care through risk-taking.

What to Do:

Attempt to stop the risk-taking behavior as you would any other undesirable behavior – by being direct, quick, and intense enough to cause some distress.

If this is not successful, the dangerous nature of this behavior may necessitate professional mental health consultation.

RUDENESS

Discussion:

Rudeness is socially unacceptable behavior (to parents or other authority figures) that basically represents anger and an ongoing test of the ability of that authority figure to be in charge of behavior.

It starts with occasional incidents that occur primarily within the immediate family. If left unchecked, such occasional incidents can spread to involve situations and adults outside the home.

What Not to Do:

Don't dismiss this behavior as "just a stage." The initial appearance may be related to a certain developmental stage, but then it develops on its own, with your child waiting (and hoping) to be effectively controlled.

Don't talk about rudeness being "bad." Rather, be specific about how this kind of behavior is not what your family believes in or does.

What to Do:

Control this behavior as soon as it presents itself, wherever, whenever, and whatever the circumstances. The younger the child, the more effective an immediate response will be.

As you respond firmly to rude behavior, be just as ready to praise desirable social behavior.

Another effective way to educate your child about your social expectations is to make a comment about other children's rudeness or lack of it.

RUNNING AWAY
Ages 5-10

Discussion:

"Serious" running away (as judged by time and distance away) is relatively rare in this age group.

It is usually an angry gesture as well as a test of the parents' love.

It is usually preceded by clear threats to run away and an obvious desire to be prevented from doing so.

An appropriate response to this behavior usually stops repeat running away and can be a valuable emotional interaction with the child.

If "serious" running away occurs, it can indicate serious emotional difficulties for the child.

What Not to Do:

Don't let anger and/or discipline be your primary response to this behavior. Never respond by threatening to remove your child from the house or family.

Don't ignore the fact that it happened or is happening. This just raises the possibility of a repeat incident.

Don't let your child know the extent to which you might have been worried, fearful, or panicked.

Don't impose restrictions on your child's activities as a consequence. That is, don't discipline for running away.

Don't allow your child to use the threat of running away as a successful method of manipulating you.

What to Do:

When your child seriously threatens to run away, say that you would be angry and that you know your child must be upset (angry, sad, etc.) to be thinking about running away.

If your child runs away, make very obvious efforts to locate and retrieve the child.

As a first response upon your child's return, show that you are glad for the return.

Then let your child know that you are angry.

Once the incident has passed, let it be forgotten. Your child will be only too glad to forget it.

Seek professional mental health consultation if the running away continues, if your child is endangered, or if the running away does not seem to be associated with emotional upset or a clear triggering event.

RUNNING AWAY
Adolescents

Discussion:

This can be a more serious situation than childhood running away, because adolescents' capabilities and knowledge allow for greater distances traveled, greater ease of "remaining lost," and a potential for more self-damaging behavior while away.

It is usually an impulsive, angry behavior, although in some cases it may be carefully planned. If the latter is the case, then the problems between the child and the parent(s) are long-standing.

In most instances the child wants to return home, if given the right opportunity to do so.

This can be a particularly upsetting experience for both parent(s) and child, as the issues of dependence/independence are important in this stage.

If handled properly, this behavior is not likely to be repeated.

If more than one child runs away, the situation is more difficult to handle.

What Not to Do:

Don't give your child time "to learn a lesson" before actively attempting to get your child home.

Don't give your child ultimatums with regard to coming home.

Don't discuss consequences of running away before your child is back.

Don't let other people give your child your message that you want a return.

Don't give your child a strong message about how upset you were or what you feared.

Don't refer to the behavior once it is over, unless your child wants to discuss it.

What to Do:

React immediately to the fact that your child has run away by a clear response of search, concern, and efforts to retrieve.

Call the police only when there is clear indication of danger to the child or when the time away becomes significant.

Indicate your willingness to discuss the situation that led to the running away.

Indicate your knowledge of how upsetting it was for your child to run away and be away.

If you feel consequences must be applied, do it after your child is back in the home and after full discussion has been allowed.

Seek professional mental health consultation if running away becomes repetitive or if the issues that caused it cannot be resolved.

SCHOOL BEHAVIOR PROBLEMS

Discussion:

This can take the form of misbehavior on the school bus, skipping classes, being disruptive in class, or not doing homework satisfactorily.

It has much more to do with things going wrong at home with you, than with anything going wrong at school.

Since good school behavior is a combination of feeling like a good child, being socially comfortable, and having a clear mind for intellectual use, then bad school behavior is a combination of the opposite.

You should assume bad school behavior does exist whenever you start getting reports about it in one form or another.

Since school behavior is a combined behavior, if it becomes bad, it is likely to get worse, unless you actively correct it.

What Not to Do:

Don't expect teachers or other school personnel to correct this behavior. Only you can truly do that.

Don't feel that any consistent or repetitive bad school behavior is "just part of growing up," etc.

Don't feel that isolated misbehavior (i.e., skipping classes while still maintaining good grades) will remain isolated. Like any other bad behavior, if it is not corrected, it will intensify and expand.

If the reports of bad behavior become repetitive, don't think that the fault is with the teacher, the school, or other children.

What to Do:

Take very seriously all reports of bad school behavior, and let your child know that you do.

Act quickly, intensively, and directly to discipline your child.

Keep in good communication with school personnel to monitor the effects of your discipline.

If your efforts are not working, seek professional mental health consultation. It is important to get any trouble corrected as soon as possible.

SECRETS AND SECRETIVE BEHAVIOR

Discussion:

The "secret" is a popular idea to the child, because it represents a form of independence from the parent. For the same reason, it is an idea that can cause discomfort, since the child wants you to have the ability to "know all."

Secrets between siblings or friends are a means of being in control, of feeling close to one another, or are a way of being competitively successful.

Secretive behavior, especially if frequent or persistent, usually represents behavior that the child thinks is bad.

What Not to Do:

Don't encourage secrets, unless they are related to something positive (like keeping secret a present or a nice surprise).

Don't encourage secrets to be held over a long period of time.

Don't interfere with secrets between your child and friends or siblings, unless it is obvious that a child is being upset or hurt by a secret.

Don't try too hard to find out secrets if your child resists telling you, unless not letting you know the secret represents bad behavior, or unless having the secret is obviously causing distress.

What to Do:

If you are comfortable with the circumstances of the secret, let your child know that you realize how much fun it can be to have a secret.

If you become aware of bad secretive behavior (sneaking out of bed late at night, playing someplace or in some way that is not allowed, smoking with friends, etc.) put an end to it as quickly as possible, in a direct fashion. It is not a good idea to become secretive, yourself, in your efforts to find out about your child's secretive behavior.

SELF-ESTEEM PROBLEMS

Discussion:

Self-esteem messages may be given verbally ("I'm not a good student."; "Other kids don't like me."; "I can't do anything right."; etc.). They may take the form of poor school performance. Or they can be seen as social isolation, reluctance to try new things, etc.

These messages are intended for you, the parent(s), in the hope that you will be able to change the feeling that the child has.

Low self-esteem is a term that includes feelings of being bad, feelings of low competence, and general sadness.

It is a condition that takes a long time to form and will take a significant effort to change.

What Not to Do:

If the low self-esteem messages are spoken, don't allow them to go unanswered.

Don't try to deny these messages or contradict them.

Don't be surprised or concerned about messages of low self-esteem that appear suddenly; they can disappear just as suddenly. You need to be concerned about the ones that are persistent and progressive.

What to Do:

If the feelings of low self-esteem are verbalized, your initial response can be to acknowledge what your child is saying and to state that it must be uncomfortable to feel this way.

If the messages keep coming, tell your child firmly that you don't want to hear that kind of talk. It may seem harsh, but actually, this is a service to your child.

If you begin to see that these messages, both verbal and behavioral, are frequent, constant, and damaging to your child's mood and/or functioning, it is important to seek professional mental health consultation.

SEPARATION AND WITHDRAWAL BEHAVIOR
Adolescents

Discussion:

There are many ways that children test your care, your control, and your knowledge about what is happening. Separating and withdrawing are a major way of testing during adolescence.

In adolescence, attempts at separating or withdrawing from you or from the family are fairly common and need to be handled properly. If not appropriately managed, this behavior can escalate.

The degree or frequency with which this type of behavior occurs depends on your response.

The withdrawal or separation can take many forms: not wanting to go on family outings; not coming to family meals on time or at all; spending hours in the bedroom; keeping the bedroom door closed most of the time; spending a lot of social time away from home.

The reason this behavior is so common at this stage is that it is based on anxiety about becoming independent — a very common concern among adolescents. It makes an adolescent angry and insecure to feel you are allowing independence (withdrawing and separating) too easily.

What Not to Do:

Don't allow your child to fool you by having "valid" reasons for being apart. It is necessary for you and the child, both, to give priority to family activities.

Don't feel that the need for privacy is more important than the need for you.

Don't feel that once you manage this behavior effectively it won't reappear. It very well might come back at a later age in another form.

What to Do:

When you recognize this behavior, give your child the message that you want him or her to spend more time with you, be away less, etc., because you want the child's company and because you care.

Be prepared for anger from your child when you start to correct this behavior. The longer the withdrawal and separation has been allowed to continue, the more intense your child's anger will be. The anger is attributable, in fact, to your not correcting the behavior sooner.

SEX QUESTIONS

Discussion:

Questions about sex are typically asked before the child becomes "sexual." They are asked when the child becomes aware that sex is somehow related to "special" or "significant" happenings: the creating of life, the fact of a new sibling, the occurrence of secretive and intense interaction between mother and father.

The effectiveness with which parents answer their child has far more significance for emotional security than it does for sexuality.

As the child will be exposed to sexual references in some form or other throughout childhood, it is important that parents' responses and information be simple and accurate. These responses will provide a basis from which the child will think about and experience sexuality in an emotionally comfortable way.

What Not to Do:

Don't give your child the idea that sexual questions are "special questions," or in any way "off limits."

Don't rely on a book to answer your child's questions. An important component of the information you provide is presenting it in your role as the child's mother or father.

Don't initiate discussion or try to give out information about sex before your child asks for it.

Try not to let any awkwardness, embarrassment, or anxiety be evident to your child during your discussion or response.

Don't let only one parent be "designated" as the information provider. Your child should get answers from whichever parent is asked.

Don't get into related discussions about morality or behavior with strangers or other children.

What to Do:

Provide as much information as your child seems to be asking for. If you decide to proceed a little further and your child loses interest or becomes anxious, that should be your cue to stop.

You should give brief, simple descriptions or answers, using the anatomical terms with which your child is familiar and uses in everyday talk.

If your child is using sexual terms you find derogatory or misinforming, you should correct the language.

Answer your child where and when asked, if possible. Attempting to find a "private place" or a "better time" may give your child a subtle message about sex that you don't intend.

SEXUAL BEHAVIOR AND EXPRESSION
Adolescents

Discussion:

Sexual behavior is important, because it involves physically pleasurable body sensations, the opportunity to be close emotionally, and a chance to compete interpersonally.

These are all-powerful factors, and any of them may be expressed as the adolescent feels the need or as circumstances allow.

The desire to experience physical pleasure can account for actions that range from masturbation and body stimulation of all kinds, to actual sexual encounters with others.

The desire to be close emotionally can account for romantic involvement, flirtation, fantasies, crushes, and a wide array of commercially produced, sexually/romantically oriented posters and magazines.

The desire to compete effectively can account for stylish or provocative dress, sexual jokes, boastful talk, social cliques.

Parents must help adolescents develop their sexuality while also helping them to remain emotionally comfortable and functional in other areas.

What Not to Do:

Don't allow sexual behavior that is extreme in any way or that violates the moral standards of the family.

If you must interrupt or control certain sexual behavior, don't say that your child is bad. Also, don't apply "loaded" labels (loose, tramp, slut, etc.) to your own child or to his or her friends.

Don't "beat around the bush" when attempting to control sexual behavior. For example, if your daughter is dressing provocatively, tell her that her dress is inappropriate or is not how you think it should be; if your son puts up sexually oriented posters in his room, tell him that they are inappropriate and not what you want to see in your house.

Don't get into a subtle but serious situation where you encourage your child's sexual behavior by showing pleasure or interest in it.

What to Do:

Remember that sexual behavior is a new behavior for your adolescent; experimentation (with anxiety and sensitivity) is to be expected. Before you become involved in any way, wait to see either extreme behavior or a pattern of unacceptable behavior.

As a general rule, the less said by you regarding acceptable sexual behavior and expression, the better.

If your adolescent girl's behavior or expression needs control, it should be mother who does the controlling.

If your adolescent boy's sexual behavior or expression needs control, it should be father who does the controlling.

SEXUAL CONTACT REPORTS

Discussion:

Reports may come from your child, either about himself/herself, or about another child, that reveal sexual contact with other children or with an adult.

These types of reports often cause great stress and anger in the parents who are hearing them. Sometimes this is a legitimate reaction, sometimes an overreaction.

These reports are always worth looking into, and they deserve the appropriate response or action.

Since children don't have a mature view of sexuality they can become confused about what is appropriate. Their reports can sound casual, whether they are reporting actual sexual abuse or normal curiosity experiences with peers.

The response that the parent makes is extremely important, since an improper response can do as much harm as the "sexual incident" itself. Conversely, a proper response may be all that is required for the child's well-being; counseling is not automatically necessary.

What Not to Do:

Don't panic when you realize that you are hearing a report about a sexual encounter. Try to appear calm and let your child finish the account before you start your questions.

You will be angry if what you hear makes you uncomfortable. Don't let anger overwhelm you. The first thing your child will think, if you are very angry, is that he or she has been bad. This is an association you want to avoid: that sexuality and being bad are linked.

Don't let anyone else get involved in the situation (other parents, police, etc.) until you have heard your child completely, have asked your questions, and are in emotional control of yourself. If other adults need to be involved in the discussion of the incident(s), try to keep your child out of it.

What to Do:

If you determine that the report represents an incident of normal sexual curiosity between children, give a response that is neutral or say that you don't want your child to "play" like that in the future.

If you determine that the report represents an incident of sexual abuse (as in a case involving an older child or an adult), let your child know: that it was good to tell about it; that the child should not be with the person again and should that person approach them they need to leave immediately and let you know about it; and that you will make sure everything will be okay. (This can include consulting with the authorities, with the child's pediatrician, or with a mental health professional.)

Once you have responded to the report and managed it, it should be discussed as the child needs to talk about it.

SHOPLIFTING

Discussion:

The act of shoplifting is more serious if it occurs when your child is alone rather than with another child or a group of children.

It is more serious if the shoplifted items are obviously not for the child's own use.

Shoplifting is often an unconscious effort on the child's part to call attention to other difficulties.

What Not to Do:

Don't let the incident go without consequences.

Don't assume it is a first step to criminal behavior.

What to Do:

Let your child know two things at once: that you are disappointed and angry, and that you are available to talk about the incident in whatever way and to whatever degree your child wants.

Seek consultation from a mental health professional if the behavior is repeated or if your child does not show appropriate distress and remorse.

SHYNESS, GENERAL DISCUSSION

Discussion:

At whatever age shyness appears, it represents the child's feeling unable to handle or process his or her current environmental situation.

Shyness is usually a behavior in which the child becomes uncomfortable – even anxious – with exposure to individual people. It may also involve discomfort with certain situations or groups of people.

Under circumstances of good development, shyness typically occurs during the process of learning about a new kind of interaction (a young baby becoming shy with strangers; an older child receiving an award in school assembly; a high school freshman at a first dance).

Shyness is a danger sign when it doesn't decrease with repeated exposure to situations that have caused anxiety, or when it is so intense that the child acts inappropriately or in extreme ways.

What Not to Do:

When you observe or become aware of the shyness, don't use negative ways of labeling it (accusing the child of acting like a baby or not having any self-confidence, etc.).

Don't try to force the child into, or through, the situation that is causing the shyness.

What to Do:

Be aware of the fact that your anger or discomfort over your child's shyness is because you have some conflict, yourself, about those same situations.

Allow the child to quietly avoid the difficult situation; don't say anything about it. Or, if your child seems to ask for some type of message from you, simply acknowledge that you know it must be a difficult situation. Then casually add the comment that it will probably get easier in the future.

SHYNESS, PUBERTY

Discussion:

The age of puberty is the age of body change. Some changes are welcome and easy to accept: increased height and strength, more mature voice, better athletic coordination.

But other changes are more difficult and can cause anxiety, embarrassment, and distress: breast enlargement, menstruation, hair growth, acne, penis erections.

Because of these difficult changes, an adolescent in puberty is likely to exhibit shyness (often sudden), sensitivity, a high degree of desire for privacy, or even social withdrawal.

This is a normal shyness and must be expected in any child at this stage.

The shyness is likely to be more evident when the child is with adults in some situations and with peers in others.

What Not to Do:

Don't comment on the difficult physical changes, unless it is necessary for the child's healthy functioning (as with straightforward education and support regarding menstrual care), or social appropriateness (such as helping your daughter buy underwear or helping your son shave).

What to Do:

If you need to make a comment, do it directly; let books be a secondary or backup method, only. Do it yourself, rather than relying on an aunt, teacher, or older sibling.

It should be the mother who talks with the daughter. It should be the father who talks with the son.

SIBLING RIVALRY

Discussion:

Although sibling rivalry or competition is inevitable, anger between siblings is not.

Persistent angry interaction is usually a sign that all is not well between one or more of the siblings and the parents. Usually competition among siblings is an attempt to get the mother's attention, rather than the father's.

Therefore, the true object of the anger is not the sibling(s), but the parents.

What Not to Do:

Don't label any particular child as the troublemaker or instigator; do not take one child's side.

Don't feel that your child's emotional well-being can be affected significantly by a sibling.

Don't imply that anger between siblings is inherently bad ("Brothers should never fight!").

Don't let the situation progress to physical harm.

What to Do:

Handle occasional anger between siblings by staying "out of it" as long or as much as possible.

Treat the situation evenhandedly, unless you actually see or hear who is at fault.

Identify the real problem between your child (or children) and you, if anger is persistent or severe.

SILENCE
Adolescents

Discussion:

Silence can represent nothing to say; anger, anxiety, or depression; or an attempt at withdrawing or separating.

Extreme silence exists when the usual degree of verbal communication and response is no longer present, or is progressively decreasing.

Short periods (a few hours to a day or two) of silence can be a normal part of adolescent development, but longer periods usually indicate a problem.

Parents can feel threatened or angered by their child's silence; however, some parents may be relieved by it.

Since parents are used to dealing with their adolescent verbally, not having this communication available may result in the parents' developing strong feelings of helplessness; they may not know what is wrong or what to do to help.

What Not to Do:

Don't try to force your child to talk. Likewise, don't ignore your child by becoming silent, yourself.

Don't let your child see your frustration and helplessness, if possible.

Don't be surprised if you discover that your child is not nearly as silent outside the home as inside. This just confirms that your child "knows" that the problem, as well as the solution, lies with you.

What to Do:

As you become aware that the silence is becoming extreme, start by casually commenting to your child about there being less talk, less communication, less response than there is normally.

Indicate that you are aware that the silence means your child is not comfortable and that you are always available for talking.

Make sure to stay in control of the situation and show your care by not allowing the silence to become a form of rude behavior or a way of separating. This may require firm emotional discipline.

SLEEP AND SLEEPING BEHAVIOR

Discussion:

From the beginning of the child's life, the time spent in sleep should become associated with routine, security, and comfort.

The quality of that sleep – the comfort and security it can provide – is greatly enhanced by the way the parents put (or send) the child to bed and the greeting they give on awakening. Also contributing are the sleep routine and the atmosphere of the bedroom.

The experience of sleep in childhood has a great bearing on the quality of sleep in adult life.

What Not to Do:

Don't provide or allow inadequate sleeping time. Babies need their naps; children need their bedtimes; and adolescents need clear expectations of sleep time.

Don't allow older children or adolescents to "take over" their bedtime and sleep routines. Always be a part of that routine, from mentioning the time, to accompanying the child to the bed, to tucking in, to kissing good night.

Don't ever believe that your child knows more about the need for sleep than you do.

What to Do:

As much as possible, set a regular and dependable routine of sleeping and bedtime. Set the same hours, in association with the same activities, the same physical contact (kissing, hugging, scratching the back) and have the same routine on awakening, a friendly greeting and a tasty breakfast.

Do a "closeness" activity associated with bedtime: stories, songs, prayers with younger children; quiet talking time (even as little as a few quick remarks) for older children and adolescents.

Make your child's bedroom a place of fun (Always have some toys and games there.) and comfort (Furnish the room with appropriate colors, decoration, bed, and other furnishings.).

Make your adolescent's bedroom appropriate, unique, private (within limits), clean, and neat.

SNACKING

Discussion:

Eating is one of the most basic ways of getting care. It provides taste pleasure, a sense of security, and an overall satisfied physical feeling.

Snacking is eating in an informal way, not at regular mealtimes, and not necessarily regular food.

If it is not excessive (does not interfere with eating regular meals, does not cause obesity, does not prevent proper nutrition), then snacking can be a valuable way of giving the child something "extra," something "special," something "instant."

Snacking is something parents can control during the child's early years. As the child's mobility, time away from home, and financial resources increase, the older child or adolescent can make snacking more of a personal choice.

What Not to Do:

Don't feel that snacking takes away from the child's good eating habits. Actually, it is an additional care experience for your child.

Don't be rigid with regard to controlling snacking (prohibiting it always at certain times; ruling out entire food groups, such as sweets etc.). In so doing, you run the risk of creating a deprivation experience for your child — something that is likely to lead to even more snacking, or even obesity.

Don't ever keep food under lock and key, or purposely out of reach. This implies distrust and is witness to your inability to apply effective emotional control.

What to Do:

If it is necessary to limit snacking at a particular time, do it by suggesting a smaller amount or even a tiny amount of whatever it is your child wants to snack on.

Provide a variety of snacks or foods suitable for snacking around the house: sweets, fruits, nuts, crackers, cookies, "junk" food, and "natural" foods.

As your child is away from the house more – whether in school, on a trip, or with friends – make sure he or she has a moderate amount of money to get a snack.

Provide snacks for your child's friends when they visit. Everyone likes to be given care.

SOCIAL PROBLEMS
Adolescents

Discussion:

The most important way that adolescents measure their success is by how successful they are socially.

This is why so much time and energy is spent trying to fit in with a group, look attractive or handsome, compete and compare, fantasize about the possibilities.

This is such a large task, and it is so difficult to be sure of the results, that it is not uncommon for a child to feel left out socially.

The degree to which a child feels left out socially can have significant effects on mood, with further effects on behavior, school functioning, and family relations.

What makes this a difficult situation for parents is the fact that information and feelings about social issues are usually kept very private by the adolescent. The child neither feels, nor has any reason to believe, that parents can be of help in this area.

What Not to Do:

Don't ask a lot of questions about your child's social life, beyond the questions that you feel are necessary for general information and control.

When you do ask occasional, casual questions about your child's social situation, don't persist or expand them if you sense any holding back, anger, or anxiety.

If you have reliable evidence that your child is being left out socially (such as not getting any phone calls, not going to school dances or other social functions, not speaking of any social interactions), don't get too upset or let your child know you are upset. A child can be "left out" or feel awkward socially at any given time, but normal development usually straightens things out before too long.

Don't try to make suggestions or "push" your child socially. This is likely to make your child feel worse.

What to Do:

Remember that social development is pretty much your child's business. Your involvement should be only in areas of control and general guidance (setting and clarifying the social standards that you approve).

If your child does decide to share feelings about the social situation, listen carefully, acknowledge positive or negative feelings, and respond that it must be nice (or difficult) to have these things happening. In addition, you may decide to ask a casual question or make a casual remark, specifically about your child's report.

SOILING PANTS
Ages 4-11

Discussion:

When a child soils his or her pants, parents must differentiate between careless or incomplete wiping and a failure to exercise bowel control.

Soiling usually represents anger in a child, as part of a child/parent conflict.

Most children who experience this difficulty are truly distressed, unhappy, and ashamed about it.

It usually occurs after school during play around the home, or on the way home from school.

Other children's awareness, comments, or teasing, are often not sufficient to resolve this difficulty.

The child may function well and otherwise appear to have no unusual difficulties.

What Not to Do:

Never ignore this situation once you have confirmed that it truly is a problem.

Try not to humiliate your child or cause embarrassment.

Don't do your child's laundry or clean up for your child.

Don't punish your child for this difficulty.

What to Do:

Let your child know that you are disappointed or unhappy with what is happening.

Try to control your anger as much as possible.

Let your child know that you realize he or she is upset inside and that maybe the anxiety is causing this difficulty.

Insist that your child be in charge of laundering the soiled clothing.

Seek professional mental health consultation as soon as possible if you realize that your own handling of the situation isn't working.

"SPOILED" BEHAVIOR

Discussion:

This is the behavior that receives frequent mention, the behavior you are warned about, the behavior that can occur with any child "if you're not careful."

It is also the behavior that is very much misunderstood.

There is, in fact, a characteristic type of behavior that deserves the label "spoiled." It is when a child is demanding, is angry, seems never to be satisfied, and seems to control the parents.

Spoiled behavior occurs when a child's needs are not being met. The popular notion is that a child becomes spoiled when given too much; in fact, it occurs when a child is not given enough.

The needs that are not being met can include a sense that the parents are not consistent, available, or in control.

Giving a child everything on demand causes spoiled behavior, not because the child is getting too much, but because of a lack of control. The child is not assured of the parents' strength, and so becomes angry and insecure. He or she becomes ever more demanding in order to test the parents' ability to control the behavior.

As unpleasant and difficult as this behavior can appear, it is fairly easily reversed.

What Not to Do:

Don't feel that "giving in" or trying to please or appease your child will make things better. It may quiet or calm your child temporarily, but it is only setting the stage to be worse at a later point.

Don't attempt to deal with the behavior by calling your child bad, spoiled, ungrateful. This is better than giving in, but it misses the point of what your child needs.

Don't think that anyone other than you, the parents, can spoil your child. They can't.

What to Do:

When you realize that your child is demanding rather than asking, is easily angered, is not satisfied with things that you give or do, you should deliberately become instantly, intensely, emotionally angry. Firmly indicate that you don't like that behavior. Repeat as often as necessary.

Continue to give the child what you wish, when you wish, and as it seems appropriate to you. You can do this as you are in the process of correcting the spoiled behavior.

Remember that any child can become "spoiled" and can test his or her parents this way at various developmental stages, from childhood through adolescence.

STEALING

Discussion:

This term should be applied to behavior where something that belongs to someone else is taken or "gotten" in a manner that the child realizes is wrong.

It is a more serious behavior (a trouble sign) if it happens repeatedly. This indicates that emotional restraint is being lost – that the stealing has become "routine" misbehavior, with all the anger, testing for control, and low self-esteem that are part of it.

It is a more serious behavior (a trouble sign) if it happens when the child is alone. This indicates that peer influence wasn't part of the explanation and that a deeper deprivation may be operating – in addition to the usual mechanisms found in "being bad."

An older child should know more, intellectually and morally, about the basic "wrongness" of stealing. Counterbalancing this awareness is the fact that there is possibly more peer pressure at this age, and a more pressing desire for the object stolen.

If the proper response is made, stealing can be effectively and quickly stopped, especially if it is not of the repetitive or individual variety. The more serious type may require professional consultation.

What Not to Do:

Once stealing is discovered, don't let the stolen item remain. In one respect, it serves as a continuing reminder of the fact of being bad. In another respect, it is a reminder of the possibility of illicitly acquiring something that is desired. Your child should take part in the actual return, if he or she is old enough (ages 8-9 and older) to benefit emotionally from the process of apologizing and restoring self-esteem.

If the stealing has occurred as part of a group activity, don't get involved with the other children or their parents; keep your handling of this behavior solely between you and your own child.

Don't spend a lot of time or energy attempting to find out, or getting your child to tell you, why the stealing occurred or under what circumstances. Just keep focused on the fact that it did occur and that it was bad.

Don't feel that restitution or reimbursement by your child is essential to an effective response. It is of secondary importance.

Don't ever feel that "time with the police" is a necessary part of an effective response. Again, this behavior is best handled by you.

What to Do:

As soon as possible, respond intensively, emotionally, and directly to your child, causing some degree of distress.

STORIES AND QUESTIONS
ABOUT EARLY YEARS

Discussion:

Well into adolescence, children are likely to ask general questions about what they were like as babies. If there are specific "baby stories" with which they have grown up, they are likely to ask that these stories be repeated.

Stories from babyhood can be very important for children to hear at certain developmental stages (when issues of independence are taking place), or at times of uncertainty or insecurity (when a new sibling comes along or when mother may be unavailable or angry).

The babyhood stories likely to be the most popular are those that show the value of the baby or a special quality that the baby had, or that illustrate that the baby was very good.

The babyhood stories that are unpopular – that children never ask about, but that parents sometimes tell – are those implying that the baby was bad in some way, or in a subtle sense, wasn't wanted or expected.

Babyhood questions are meant to elicit reassuring answers, or to let the child imagine being a baby who was desirable in a certain way.

Typical questions are:
"Was I a good baby?"
"What was my favorite toy?"
"What was my favorite food?"
"Did you feel badly when I hurt myself?"
"Did you stay with me when I was in the hospital?"
"Did Daddy like to take me to work with him?"

What Not to Do:

Don't tell babyhood stories that your child never asks about or that don't seem to give pleasure.

Don't say that your child is too old to be asking about babyhood.

Don't always answer questions in a truthful fashion. Leave out or change facts that don't sound generally positive.

Don't worry about stories – or answers to questions – that grandparents, neighbors, etc., tell. They don't have much real emotional impact on your child, because they don't come from you, the parent.

What to Do:

Give generally positive answers to babyhood questions and use appropriate opportunities to tell "favorite" babyhood stories.

SUICIDAL AND SELF-DESTRUCTIVE MESSAGES

Discussion:

Suicide or suicide attempts are a result of depression, a sense of hopelessness, a need for care. The actual self-destructive behavior is not truly intended to cause physical harm or death, but to elicit care.

Therefore, the most effective response to suicidal messages is one that promises care, in the form of hope and effective control.

Since care is what is being sought, suicidal thinking or ideas will not be kept secret. They will become obvious through behavior, talk, or written messages.

Many situations where children harm or kill themselves occur accidentally. The child wants care, not pain or death. In instances where suicide is attempted, the self-destructive messages simply weren't recognized or effectively answered.

It may seem difficult to decide what are actually serious or significant self-destructive messages.

It is safest and simplest to regard seriously any messages from a child that refer to feeling: hopeless, in danger, like "putting an end" to things, self-destructive, etc.

What Not to Do:

Don't minimize, or ignore, self-destructive messages (talk, behavior, written messages).

Don't spend a lot of time trying to talk your child out of the feelings, or trying to convince him or her that things aren't really so bad. You can try this briefly, but for a truly depressed child, it won't work.

Don't react to self-destructive messages with either anger or expressions of helplessness. Neither will reassure your child about your care or control.

Don't try to "scare your child out of it" by saying what could happen or what has happened to others who attempted suicide.

Don't give the impression that you don't believe your child is really serious about the messages, or that he or she is just "looking for attention."

What to Do:

Tell your child, seriously and firmly, that you regard this behavior as dangerous, but that you hear clearly what has been said or written.

Also, mention that you know how very uncomfortable it must be to have these thoughts or to act this way.

If these ways of responding do not stop the messages, consult a mental health professional. You must make the decision to do this as soon as you begin to become aware of the seriousness of the situation. Your child wants you to be in charge of basic care. Act sooner, not later.

SWEARING

Discussion:

In a child, swearing is the use of words that are clearly out of keeping with the family standards. The child knows the language is unacceptable.

Swearing gets started for its own developmental reasons. Then, like other "bad behavior," it clearly serves the purpose of testing the parents for care through control.

Swearing in a younger child (ages 8-11) – especially in boys – is started in an attempt to feel powerful, as these words are associated with older males.

Swearing in an adolescent usually reflects an effort to fit in with a group socially – to use the language of the group.

Since an adolescent is more aware of family standards, parental failure to control swearing in this age group is likely to result in anger, insecurity, and a need to keep testing for control. Hence, more swearing.

What Not to Do:

Don't let even one swear word "slip by" without your appropriate response.

Don't feel like a hypocrite if you occasionally swear (such as when you are angry or frustrated). Your child can be very comfortable with a "double standard," if you are comfortable, because you are the parent.

Don't feel you have to stop the swearing your child may practice when alone with friends. In fact, it shows good development (and good parental control) if your child can use one type of language with friends and a different one within the family.

What to Do:

When you hear a swear word, tell your child immediately and firmly, that this kind of language is not allowed in the family.

TALKATIVENESS, EXTREME

Discussion:

The purpose of talking is to communicate.

When talking becomes rapid, constant, and clearly beyond the realm of communication needs, it is probably serving the purpose of anxiety reduction. There is some security in the sound of one's own voice and the structure of saying something. It may be a necessary developmental activity (a young child mastering new concepts and words; an adolescent verbalizing concepts of a confusing world).

Extreme talkativeness can be a problem for the adult(s) around the child, because: of the noise involved, the real or perceived need to talk a lot in response to the child, or the sense that the child is not comfortable.

What Not to Do:

Don't let your only response to this talkativeness be that of anger (irritation, frustration, impotence, etc.). If you find yourself becoming angry, try to separate yourself from your child or your child from you.

Don't forget that this behavior tends to be limited by time and developmental circumstances. Chances are it won't go on too long or become much worse.

Don't label your child because of the behavior (chatterbox, magpie, etc.).

Don't change your style of talking in order to interact verbally with your talkative child.

What to Do:

Be patient and indicate to your child that you are listening (by nodding, grunting, or inserting an occasional word).

If you can find a natural opportunity to do so, indicate in an age-appropriate way that your child seems to have a lot to say. Making your child more aware of this kind of behavior speeds its disappearance.

TANTRUMS

Discussion:

Tantrums are expressions of anger, usually caused by the child's not getting his or her "own way."

Not having much experience with language, nor the maturity to tolerate frustration, the young child uses the tantrum almost automatically as a way of reacting.

The child is upset by this behavior. Accordingly, tantrums tend to "feed on themselves."

What Not to Do:

If your child is having a tantrum, don't give what your child seems to want.

Don't alternate between trying to please your child and getting angry with your child.

Don't "walk out" on your child.

Don't forget that this type of behavior is a normal and necessary way in which your child learns to "deal with the world."

Don't refer back to the tantrum once it is finished.

What to Do:

Allow the tantrum to go on for a few minutes.

Then firmly tell your child to stop. If that doesn't work, use your voice tone to threaten your child. Finally, you might have to spank your child on the buttocks with your hand (Infliction of pain is not necessary; shock value is what counts).

Once your child ends the tantrum and is crying, hug and hold him or her firmly. If the tantrum starts again, respond the same way again.

TARDINESS
Young Children

Discussion:

Tardiness of young children is only a matter of the parent's perception. The child operates within a time frame with no deadlines. Therefore, a sense of speed or tardiness is determined by the parent in the early years.

The degree to which the child associates being tardy with being bad will determine whether tardiness persists into later years and how much of a problem it causes in effective functioning.

It is the combination of a child's motor/perceptive development, plus an innate desire to please the parent(s), that best contributes to efficient and timely behavior.

What Not to Do:

Don't let your impatience (anger) about your child's tardiness affect your verbal or physical efforts to speed up things. Angry words or rough handling only contribute to the child's sense of being bad.

Don't walk away angrily or threaten to leave your child behind because of tardiness or slowness. Again, the threatened loss of you or your love quickly translates in your child's mind to the fact of being bad.

Don't attempt to speed up things by just using words. Helping out, showing, or picking up the child can be far more effective.

Don't use verbal expressions of lateness or lost time for your children. The concept of time lost is not easily or comfortably grasped before ages 4 to 6.

What to Do:

Praise your child's efforts and ability to do things, perform tasks, and move quickly. This develops a sense of being good in this context.

When you need to give a message about speeding up things, use examples with which your child is familiar (quick like a bunny, fast as Superman, etc.).

Remember that your child, as part of efforts to feel competent, will naturally do things as quickly as development allows.

TARDINESS
Adolescents

Discussion:

When adolescents are tardy, slow-moving, or even stationary on a regular basis, it usually reflects anxiety or anger. Since they have the physical ability to move more quickly, and since they have a better-developed time sense, tardiness is clearly caused by emotions.

If your adolescent feels like a bad person in other respects, then tardiness is associated with anger, and the general purpose is to test your care and your ability to be in control.

If the activity or task at hand is one that is associated with physical or social development or interaction, then anxiety is the emotional cause of the tardiness.

If the tardiness is of the bad/angry/testing variety, it needs to be handled quickly and effectively. Properly handled, it will soon disappear.

If the tardiness is of the anxiety/developmental variety, then your responses and understanding are crucial to your child's comfort.

What Not to Do:

Don't become too impatient with the occasional or sporadic tardiness of your child. It goes with the stage and represents normal development (in the general categories of assertion, independence, or regression).

Don't refer to your child as "bad" and don't make reference to other "bad behavior" as you are attempting to speed up your child.

Don't ask many questions like "What is taking you so long?" More often than not, your child can't put into words what is going on, anyway. Instead, be clear and direct that your child is taking too long and needs to be faster.

Don't assume, based on prior experience, that your child will be tardy. Address this behavior only if it is actually occurring.

Don't "characterize" your child as tardy in a joking way or in social settings. Labeling will only cause or intensify anger.

What to Do:

If the tardiness is of the anxiety/developmental variety (your adolescent girl who takes hour-long showers, your adolescent boy who takes hours to mow the lawn), try to be flexible with your expectations or the household routine. Be liberal with your praise and appreciation when the pace quickens, and be optimistic about the temporary nature of the tardy behavior.

If the tardiness is of the bad/angry/testing variety (your adolescent who is routinely late for dinner, or who is routinely late for school), respond with your anger and demand for change. Do so directly and as quickly as possible after each incidence of tardiness.

TATTLETALES

Discussion:

A child is most comfortable when he or she feels like a good person, or when parents are aware of bad behavior. Therefore, if a child is aware that another child is being bad (whether in the family, in the classroom, or in play situations), that child will usually try to make the appropriate authority aware of the bad behavior.

This is why telling tales takes place. It is for a good reason — an attempt to remain comfortable. However, a child who gets a reputation as a tattletale has problems. First, it indicates that he or she is very sensitized to issues of "bad" and "good" and probably feels more like a bad child than a good one. Second, such behavior tends to make the child unpopular with peers, since it is the tattler who is responsible for reprimands or discipline being doled out to those peers.

This type of behavior usually does not occur in adolescence, because peer approval is far more powerful at this stage.

What Not to Do:

Don't do anything to stop the occasional tattler. Remember, there is a good reason for its happening.

Don't attempt to stop tattling just by saying that telling tales isn't nice. Rather, indicate that you know that the tattler didn't like seeing or being around bad behavior and that you are sure the appropriate "authority" (mother, teacher, etc.) will find out and take the proper action.

What to Do:

If telling tales seems to be happening frequently, let your child know that you are aware he or she really seems to notice, and be bothered by, bad behavior. This interpretive response will effectively reduce tattling.

TEASING

Discussion:

Teasing is an expression of anger which is directed toward a quality, condition, or behavior of the person being teased.

The reason teasing occurs is that the other person's quality, condition, or behavior is making the teaser uncomfortable in some way. When someone is uncomfortable, that person is likely to become angry.

The child being teased is in some way making the teaser uncomfortable and, thus, angry.

An example is the boy who is teased for being a "sissy" (another word for weakness). Since boys like to feel strong, they may find themselves very uncomfortable around a child who appears or acts weakly. It makes them angry, and the anger is directed, in the form of teasing, toward the source of their discomfort, "the sissy."

A certain amount of teasing and being teased is part of normal development. There is cause for concern, however, if a child teases or is teased a lot.

If there is a lot of teasing between siblings, it can be a sign that something is not right between one or more of the children and the parents. (See the chapter on sibling rivalry.)

What Not to Do:

If your child talks a lot about being teased, don't ignore it, don't deny it, don't encourage your child to "tease the other child (children) back."

If you discover that your child is teasing others a lot, don't ignore it or excuse it.

What to Do:

If your child talks a lot about being teased, indicate that you are listening, and that it must be difficult to have that happen. That should be the limit of your response. If you feel that there is more to be done to keep your child comfortable, call teachers or parents to let them know what is happening, so that your child can be protected.

If you find out that your child is teasing others a lot, let yourself become appropriately, emotionally angry and insist upon a stop to this bad behavior.

If there is a lot of teasing between your own children, try to find out why there is anger toward you. If the teasing between your children seems moderate, let them settle it themselves and only intervene when one child really seems to be getting hurt, emotionally or physically.

TESTING THE PARENT UNIT

Discussion:

Children need guidance and control. When both are clear and consistent, the child is secure.

Although there are two parents, there should, ideally, be only one set of guidelines and one method of control. The parents should act as a unit.

Parental unity is a reassuring fact to a child. It eliminates the need to test that unity or to separate the parents.

Testing parents to see if they agree occurs when they give the children inconsistent or incompatible messages. Such testing eminates from the hope that consistency will somehow occur.

Attempts to separate parents is typical of certain developmental stages, but is ultimately a request from the child for reassurance that the parents can't be separated.

What Not to Do:

Don't continue with messages, responses, or discipline that you, as parents, clearly disagree about. Inevitably, the child will become aware of the disagreement.

Don't argue or disagree with your spouse about the method of handling a situation, either in front of, or within hearing distance of, your child.

Don't let your child try to divide the parental unit by complaining about the other parent. You can allow your child to talk, but simply say that you are listening only, not judging.

What to Do:

Frequent references such as "your mother and I" or "Daddy

and I" are reassuring to your child and help to reduce the need to test "the unit."

If control or discipline occurs with only one parent present, the incident should be made known to the other parent. The other parent, in turn, should let the child know in some way (not necessarily by disciplining all over again) that he or she is aware of what has happened.

One parent should not be "in charge" of discipline exclusively. In a subtle way, this encourages your child to think that the inactive parent is not really an effective partner in the parent unit.

TOMBOY BEHAVIOR
Adolescent Girls

Discussion:

This behavior is most easily characterized as a girl being clearly "unfeminine" in dress, grooming, and especially, athletic activity.

If acting like a "tomboy" is a stage of healthy development it will typically disappear by age 16 or 17.

Being a "tomboy" is a clever – though subconscious – way of safely being close to father (or other males), while not being competitive with mother (or other females).

It is such a common condition, that there are lots of other "tomboy" girls with which to socialize.

What Not to Do:

Don't attempt to change this behavior. It serves too important a purpose.

Don't lose sight of the fact that this is a more healthy and more comfortable way of passing through early adolescence than being precociously feminine.

What to Do:

Support your daughter's athletic involvement. Let father become especially active. This is a good way (it may be the only way for a while) for him to be close.

During this tomboy period, mother should gently and persistently encourage the daughter's femininity.

UNHAPPY BABY

Discussion:

An unhappy baby is typically hard to hold, not content, and apparently in distress.

All mothers are sensitive to this type of behavior. Some are too sensitive.

Difficulty and uncertainty in this situation may lead to increasingly interdependent unhappiness between mother and her baby.

Often, there are physical factors responsible.

This situation is more likely to occur with an inexperienced or depressed mother than with one who has other children or who is in good spirits.

What Not to Do:

Don't deal angrily with your baby out of frustration.

Don't ignore your baby.

Don't ask for advice from too many people who are not specialists.

Don't hesitate to talk to your pediatrician or family doctor.

What to Do:

Keep smiling and talking quietly to your baby.

Keep touching and holding your baby.

Ask an experienced mother to observe you with your baby.

Eliminate any physical causes with the aid of your pediatrician.

WORRYING AND OTHER SAFETY CONCERNS

Discussion:

This is a situation where a child will verbalize, frequently or intensely, worries about various environmental issues (the house catching fire, earthquakes, nuclear war) or personal issues (getting lost, getting sick, a grandparent dying).

The common factors in any of these expressed worries are a sense of vulnerability and the desire to elicit parents' response and reassurance.

Often these worries are triggered (not caused) by an actual event that the child has experienced or just heard about.

What Not to Do:

Don't try to convince your child that the worry or concern doesn't make sense or that the thing causing concern couldn't happen.

Don't ridicule your child or label him or her a "worrier."

Don't change plans or do things differently based on these expressed worries.

Don't present reassuring comments in an effort to prevent the worries until your child expresses concerns.

Don't respond angrily or indicate any sense of helplessness.

What to Do:

Let your child know that you hear, and that you recognize that having those kinds of worries must be difficult.

Keep repeating the above, even though your child tries to get you to respond to the specifics of his or her concerns. If necessary, firmly tell your child that you do not want to hear any more at this time. This does work; it subtly conveys the idea that there is, indeed, nothing to worry about.

If this type of response does not seem to be controlling the worries, it may be necessary to consult with a mental health professional.

WRITING: JOURNAL, MESSAGE & LETTER
Adolescents

Discussion:

Writing is an activity that represents an important aspect of adolescent development – expression of feelings.

In the adolescent years, feelings can be conveyed in writing more easily than through the spoken word.

Also, feelings on paper can be shared with friends, read over and over again, sent long distances or short, or put away into secret places for personal review at a future time.

Another important purpose of written messages – though your child is hardly aware of it – is to tell you, the parent, something, or let you know what is happening. This is why notes, letters, or journals are often left lying around, in places guaranteed to attract your attention.

What Not to Do:

Don't ask to read these personal written messages, and don't open your child's mail.

If messages are left around "begging to be read," read them in private – never in front of your child – return them to their original place and then keep all the information to yourself. If you read about negative or naughty behavior, store away the information and use it to better manage or respond to your child. Only if what you read is truly outrageous, immoral, or unsafe should you confront your child about it.

What to Do:

Respect your child's privacy when he or she is reading or writing a message. You can even suggest or provide a private place to keep such personal written things.

Mention something casually about your child's writing or receiving a written message, to show that you are aware of this very important part of his or her life.